Rhetorical Studies of National Political Debates—1996

Recent Titles in the
Praeger Series in Political Communication
Robert E. Denton, Jr., General Editor

Rhetorical Studies of National Political Debates—1996

Edited by
Robert V. Friedenberg

Praeger Series in Political Communication

PRAEGER

Westport, Connecticut
London

Library of Congress Cataloging-in-Publication Data

Rhetorical studies of national political debates—1996 / edited by
Robert V. Friedenberg.
    p. cm.—(Praeger series in political communication, ISSN
1062–5623)
    Includes bibliographical references and index.
    ISBN 0–275–95738–1 (pbk. : alk. paper)
    1. Presidents—United States—Election—1996. 2. United States—
Politics and government—1993– 3. Campaign debates—United States—
History—20th century. 4. Communication in politics—United
States—History—20th century. 5. Rhetoric—Political aspects—
United States—History—20th century. I. Friedenberg, Robert V.
II. Series.
E888.R47   1997
324.973'0929—DC21   97–14470

British Library Cataloguing in Publication Data is available.

Library of Congress Catalog Card Number: 97–14470
ISBN: 0–275–95738–1 (pbk.)
ISSN: 1062–5623

First published in 1997

Praeger Publishers, 88 Post Road West, Westport, CT 06881
An imprint of Greenwood Publishing Group, Inc.

Printed in the United States of America

The paper used in this book complies with the
Permanent Paper Standard issued by the National
Information Standards Organization (Z39.48–1984).

P

In order to keep this title in print and available to the academic community, this edition
was produced using digital reprint technology in a relatively short print run. This would
not have been attainable using traditional methods. Although the cover has been changed
from its original appearance, the text remains the same and all materials and methods
used still conform to the highest book-making standards.

Contents

Series Foreword

Those of us from the discipline of communication studies have long believed that communication is prior to all other fields of inquiry. In several other forums I have argued that the essence of politics is "talk" or human interaction.[1] Such interaction may be formal or informal, verbal or nonverbal, public or private, but it is always persuasive, forcing us consciously or subconsciously to interpret, to evaluate, and to act. Communication is the vehicle for human action.

From this perspective, it is not surprising that Aristotle recognized the natural kinship of politics and communication in his writings *Politics* and *Rhetoric*. In the former, he establishes that humans are "political beings [who] alone of the animals [are] furnished with the faculty of language."[2] And in the latter, he begins his systematic analysis of discourse by proclaiming that "rhetorical study, in its strict sense, is concerned with the modes of persuasion."[3] Thus, it was recognized over 2,300 years ago that politics and communication go hand in hand because they are essential parts of human nature.

Back in 1981, Dan Nimmo and Keith Sanders proclaimed that political communication was an emerging field.[4] Although its origin, as noted, dates back centuries, a "self-consciously cross-disciplinary" focus began in the late 1950s. Thousands of books and articles later, colleges and universities offer a variety of graduate and undergraduate coursework in the area in such diverse departments as communication, mass communication, journalism, political science, and sociology.[5] In Nimmo and Sanders' early assessment, the "key areas of inquiry" included rhetorical analysis, propaganda analysis, attitude change studies, voting studies, government and the news media, functional and systems analyses, technological changes, media technologies, campaign techniques, and research techniques.[6] In a survey of the state of the field in 1983, the same authors and Lynda Kaid found additional, more specific areas of concern such as the presidency, political polls, public opinion, debates, and advertising, to name a few.[7] Since the first study, they also noted a shift away from the rather strict behavioral approach.

A decade later, Dan Nimmo and David Swanson argued that "political communication has developed some identity as a more or less distinct domain of scholarly work."[8] The scope and concerns of the area have further expanded to include critical theories and cultural studies. While there is no precise definition, method, or disciplinary home of the area of inquiry, its primary domain is the role, processes, and effects of communication within the context of politics broadly defined.

In 1985, the editors of *Political Communication Yearbook: 1984* noted that "more things are happening in the study, teaching, and practice of political communication that can be captured within the space limitations of the relatively few publications available."[9] In addition, they argued that the backgrounds of "those involved in the field [are] so varied and pluralist in outlook and approach, . . . it [is] a mistake to adhere slavishly to any set format in shaping the content."[10] And more recently, Nimmo and Swanson called for "ways of overcoming the unhappy consequences of fragmentation within a framework that respects, encourages, and benefits from diverse scholarly commitments, agendas, and approaches.[11]

In agreement with these assessments of the area and with gentle encouragement, Praeger established the Praeger Series in Political Communication. The series is open to all qualitative and quantitative methodologies as well as contemporary and historical studies. The key to characterizing the studies in the series is the focus on communication variables or activities within a political context or dimension. As of this writing, nearly 40 volumes have been published, and there are numerous impressive works forthcoming. Scholars from the disciplines of communication, history, journalism, political science, and sociology have participated in the series.

I am, without shame or modesty, a fan of the series. The joy of serving as its editor is in participating in the dialogue of the field of political communication and in reading the contributors' works. I invite you to join me.

Robert E. Denton, Jr.

NOTES

1. See Robert E. Denton, Jr., *The Symbolic Dimensions of the American Presidency* (Prospect Heights, Ill.: Waveland Press, 1982); Robert E. Denton, Jr., and Gary Woodward, *Political Communication in America* (New York: Praeger, 1985; 2nd ed., 1990); Robert E. Denton, Jr., and Dan Han, *Presidential Communication* (New York: Praeger, 1986); and Robert E. Denton, Jr., *The Primetime Presidency of Ronald Reagan* (New York: Praeger, 1988).

2. Aristotle, *The Politics of Aristotle*, trans. Ernest Barker (New York: Oxford University Press, 1970), p. 5.

3. Aristotle, *Rhetoric*, trans. Rhys Roberts (New York: The Modern Library, 1954), p. 22.

4. Dan Nimmo and Keith Sanders, "Introduction: The Emergence of Political Communication as a Field," in *Handbook of Political Communication*, ed. Dan Nimmo and Keith Sanders (Beverly Hills, Calif.: Sage, 1981), pp. 11–36.

5. Ibid., p. 15.

6. Ibid., pp. 17–27.

7. Keith Sanders, Lynda Kaid, and Dan Nimmo, eds., *Political Communication Yearbook: 1984* (Carbondale: Southern Illinois University, 1985), pp. 283–308.

8. Dan Nimmo and David Swanson, "The Field of Political Communication: Beyond the Voter Persuasion Paradigm," in *New Directions in Political Communication*, ed. David Swanson and Dan Nimmo (Beverly Hills, Calif.: Sage, 1990), p. 8.

9. Sanders, Kaid, and Nimmo, *Political Communication Yearbook: 1984,* p. xiv.

10. Ibid.

11. Nimmo and Swanson, "The Field of Political Communication," p. 11.

Introduction

Robert V. Friedenberg

Seventeen of the most widely seen and heard speakers in history all have one thing in common. They were all seen and heard while engaged in national political debates as they sought the two highest offices Americans can bestow upon their countrymen. This book focuses on the most recent four of those individuals and the rhetorical centerpieces of their respective campaigns, the 1996 political campaign debates.

From ancient Greece and Rome to the present, free societies have relied upon the vigorous clash of ideas in an open and free marketplace of ideas as a means of decision making. American society reflects that clash of ideas at virtually every key point in its history. America was born in the clash between Whig and Tory primarily from 1763 to 1776. A sick nation was nurtured to health in the clash of the Constitutional Convention of 1787. Repeatedly, the clash of ideas has characterized American decision making. Most often, those clashes have taken place either in legislative proceedings or in political campaigns.

Political debates, face-to-face confrontations between two candidates, were non-existent in national political elections prior to 1960, though they were relatively common in campaigns for lesser offices. Rather, most of the clash found in national political campaigns was in the form of a single speech or series of speeches by one candidate which generated a response from a second candidate. Often, that response generated yet another response from the first candidate and the clash continued. But the candidates might be miles apart and the speeches separated in time by days or weeks. Audiences might have a sense of the flow of ideas, but it was often difficult to compare the candidates and their positions closely. Additionally, prior to 1960 surrogate debates were also an occasional feature of national campaigns. But surrogates are not the candidates themselves, and such debates often generated little attention and did little to facilitate candidate comparisons.

In 1960, the decisions of Senator John F. Kennedy and Vice President Richard M. Nixon to participate in a series of joint appearances, combined with the growth of the still young television industry, enabled Kennedy and Nixon to be observed simultaneously by vast audiences while debating the issues of the day. Although one might question whether these appearances were in fact debates, none could question that the face of contemporary American political campaigning would never be the same.

Although it took sixteen years for two more presidential candidates to agree to debate, joint appearances similar to the Kennedy-Nixon debates were frequently utilized in races for lesser offices. By 1976, when Governor Jimmy Carter and President Gerald Ford decided to debate, it was natural that their vice presidential candidates, Senators Walter Mondale and Robert Dole, also debated.

In the years since Kennedy and Nixon stood before the American public, political debates, at the national level, have become virtually institutionalized. When Kennedy and Nixon chose to debate, they in fact *chose* to debate. Today, the pressures to debate imposed by a society expecting the principal candidates for the highest offices in the nation to clash in a debate or quasi-debate format are so great that, as the essays in the prior companion volume to this one, *Rhetorical Studies of National Political Debates: 1960–1992* illustrate, the decision to debate is no longer exclusively in the hands of the candidates themselves.[1]

While the individual debates treated in these pages will no doubt be subject to extensive study, this volume brings together the work of scholars with strong interests in political communication and debate. Like the contributors to the prior companion volume, Professors Kathleen Kendall and Gaut Ragsdale were asked to focus on (1) the factors motivating the candidates to debate, (2) the goals of each candidate in debating, (3) the rhetorical strategies utilized by each candidate, and (4) the effects of the debate. The concluding chapter of this book is the editor's updated expansion, drawing on the work of Professors Kendall and Ragsdale, to provide up-to-date insight into patterns and trends of national political debating.[2]

By allowing skilled rhetorical critics to focus on the most recent of our national political debates, in a fashion compatible with similar studies of every national debate held since 1960, this volume should serve two purposes. First, it should add to our understanding of each of these two most recent debates. Professor Kendall, recognizing that most Americans draw their impressions of political debates heavily from the televised treatment of the debates themselves and the surrounding news stories, provides readers with an examination of the rhetoric of the 1996 debates as a televised event. Professor Ragsdale has focused his examination of the vice presidential debates on the rhetoric itself, providing readers with insight gained from a close examination of the text and the thoughts of several of those immediately involved with the debate. Second, this volume should serve to place the 1996 debates in the context of almost 40 years of national political debates, helping readers to perceive trends and patterns in national political campaign debating. The final chapter represents the editor's attempt to fulfill this second purpose of this volume.

At the conclusion of the final 1960 debate, moderator Quincy Howe of ABC News observed that "as members of a new political generation, Vice President Nixon and Senator Kennedy have used new means of communication to pioneer a new type of political debate. The character and courage with which these two men have spoken sets a high standard for generations to come. Surely they have set a new precedent. Perhaps they have established a new tradition."[3] Today we know that they did indeed establish a new tradition. To the extent that this volume contributes to a better understanding of that tradition, it will have served a valuable function.

NOTES

1. See Robert V. Friedenberg, "Trends and Patterns in National Political Debates: 1960–1992," in *Rhetorical Studies of National Political Debates: 1960–1992*, ed. Robert V. Friedenberg (Westport, Conn.: Praeger, 1994), pp. 236–240.

2. Ibid., pp. 235–260.

3. *The Joint Appearances of Senator John F. Kennedy and Vice President Richard M. Nixon. Presidential Campaign of 1960* (Washington D.C.: U.S. Government Printing Office, 1961), p. 278.

Rhetorical
Studies of National
Political Debates—1996

Chapter 1

The 1996 Clinton-Dole Presidential Debates: Through Media Eyes

Kathleen E. Kendall

The presidential debates came to national attention in the age of television. Beginning with the Kennedy-Nixon debates of 1960, millions of Americans have watched them on television. Not only do they see the debates, but they also see the commentary about those debates on television news, as well as in other media. Many more people who have not watched the debates also hear or read analyses of them. This chapter focuses on the way television news covered the presidential debates of 1996.[1]

There is much evidence of the influence of the media's interpretation of debates. Studies comparing the perceptions of viewers exposed to post-debate commentary with those not exposed have established that the groups differ significantly in their impressions of which candidate did the better job. Those who saw the news commentary are more likely to agree with the news verdict.[2] Media interpretations have been found to follow a pattern: they devote little time to the content of the debates, and much time to the personalities of the candidates and the process by which they make the decision to debate, prepare to debate, and "spin" the stories about expectations for and effects of the debate. These interpretations are usually cast in the framework of a horse race, seeing the debate as a dramatic contest of real importance to the candidates, and expressing most interest in the question, "Who won?" They rely heavily on instant polls to answer that question.[3]

In covering political speeches in general, the media frequently mention the speeches of presidential candidates, but cast them in a subordinate role, as a form of proof for wider claims. In Kendall's study of network coverage of speeches and debates by presidential candidates in the 1992 primary campaign period, only one speech received a lead story by one of the national networks: the State of the Union address. The networks seldom let the candidates speak for themselves, instead digesting and recasting the speech in the words of the reporter. The result of this presentation of speeches on the news was a trivializing of their substance and a flattening and neutralizing of their style.[4]

Since presidential debates are a form of speech, the expectation in this study was that the media would cover the presidential debates in the fall campaign in much the same way as the primary campaign speeches. The one significant difference in the situation is that the presidential debates in the fall are generally televised in full on the national networks and viewed by millions, while primary debates and speeches are not as widely accessible. The findings of the Kendall 1993 study led to the following hypotheses:[5]

1. That there would be many lead stories about the presidential campaign, but not about the debates;
2. That the debates would be mentioned frequently within the framework of the campaign story;
3. That the candidates' own words in the debates would seldom be shown, and if shown would be very brief;
4. That the debates would be described primarily in the words of the journalists;
5. That the networks would discuss the debates chiefly as a form of proof to back up wider claims about the campaign.

In addition to examining these hypotheses, the author also asked three questions similar to those examined in all the essays edited by Friedenberg (1994). The questions are as follows:

1. How did the media present the goals of each candidate in the debates?
2. How did the media present the rhetorical strategies utilized by each candidate in the debates?
3. How did the media present the effects of the debates?

METHODS

Network news coverage of the presidential debates in the 1996 general election campaign was examined for a 25-day period from one week before the debates began on September 29 until one week after they ended on October 23. The programs included ABC's *World News Tonight*, NBC's *Nightly News*, CBS's *Evening News*, and CNN's *Prime Time*. One of the network broadcasts was viewed for each date, in random order every four days so as to include an equal number from each network. On the days following the presidential debates (Oct. 7 and 17), the news was viewed on all four networks. In this way, 31 evening news reports were sampled for the content analysis, 8 from ABC, 8 from CBS, 8 from NBC, and 7 from CNN.

In addition, the post-debate news specials were viewed on all four networks on the debate nights (Oct. 6 and 16). Reading of debate coverage in the *New York Times* and the Albany *Times Union* also provided contextual information.

Methods were replicated from the Kendall 1993 study.[6] All lead stories were transcribed to ascertain how many of them focused on the campaign and if any dealt with debates. This would help indicate how much emphasis the networks gave to debates in the campaign. The number and order of campaign news stories in each broadcast were recorded, as well as the number and order of stories about the debates, whether lead stories or subordinate stories within the framework of the campaign story. The debate stories were the units of analysis. They included scenes of the debate setting, of candidates debating or discussing the debates, interviews with the candidates' staffs, audience members viewing the debates, debate experts discussing the debates, polls on debate effects, and commentary by reporters and anchors. Lead stories on the debates were recorded and timed from start to finish. All debate excerpts were recorded verbatim, and notes were taken on the reporters' comments and the visual aspects of the portrayals, including context.

RESULTS

In the 31 news stories examined, the networks discussed the presidential campaign in 30 stories, or 97 percent of the time. The debates were mentioned in 21 of the 31 stories, or 68 percent of the time. The campaign in general accounted for nine lead stories (29%), and the debates accounted for seven additional lead stories (23%). The debates were also discussed within the leading campaign story five times, or 16 percent. Thus, the debates were the subject of the lead story or part of the lead story a total of 39 percent of the time. If one excludes the eight stories on the nights after the presidential debates (Oct. 7 and Oct. 17), four of the lead stories focused on the debates (17%), and two general campaign stories contained discussion of the debates, for a total of 26 percent of the nightly coverage on the debates.

Hypothesis 1 was therefore supported in its first part but not in its second part. There were many lead stories about the presidential campaign, as expected. What was not expected was that there would also be many lead stories about the presidential debates themselves.

Hypothesis 2 was supported. The debates were mentioned frequently within the framework of the campaign story. In the post-debate specials, the programs in their entirety were devoted to discussion of the debate on ABC, CBS, and NBC. CNN adopted a novel approach: rather than discussing the just-completed debates, Larry King interviewed Ross Perot and the candidates of four minor parties, asking them some of the same questions posed in the presidential debates.

The placement and length of the debate stories in this period followed a clear pattern on the nightly news. Five of the seven lead stories on the debates occurred mainly before or after the first presidential debate. There was also one the night of the vice presidential debate, and one the night of the second presidential debate. The first presidential debate was the subject of the longest news stories: CNN devoted 10 minutes on October 5 (lead story), CBS devoted 8 minutes 48 seconds on October 6 (lead story), and on October 7, the night after the first debate, the times were: NBC, 8 minutes 42 seconds (lead); ABC, 7 minutes 17 seconds (lead); CBS, 6 minutes 1 second (lead); CNN, 3 minutes 25 seconds (second story). One other long lead story occurred on NBC the night of the second debate. It was 5 minutes 57 seconds long. On the night after the second debate there was less time devoted to the debate, and no specific lead stories. The last six evening newscasts examined, October 18–23, did not mention the debates, with the exception of the October 19 CNN story about post-debate poll findings.

The post-debate specials occurred immediately after the presidential and vice presidential debates ended, on October 6, 9, and 16 on all four networks. The average length of the programs on ABC, CBS, and NBC (excluding advertisements) was 17 minutes, with CNN devoting 90 minutes to the minor party candidates.

Hypothesis 3, that the candidates' own words in the debates would seldom be shown, and if shown would be very brief, was supported. There is one caveat, however. All four networks showed the debates in their entirety. This was a major commitment of time—90 minutes—to the candidates' own words. In the news coverage of the debates, however, there was little of the candidates speaking in the debates. Kendall found, in her primaries study, that networks showed candidate speeches on 62 percent of the evenings.[7] In the 31 news stories examined in this study, only four stories (CBS, Oct. 7; NBC, Oct. 7; CNN, Oct. 12; ABC, Oct. 17) showed the candidates speaking in the debate. This amounts to only 13 percent of the stories, and totalled a mere 33 seconds. Most of this time was accounted for by a 26-second "Reality Check" of the debates by Erik Engberg of CBS on October 7. A fourth story (ABC, Oct. 17) showed pictures only (no sound) from the debate, for 8 seconds. There were also two stories which presented excerpts from historical debates: a long discussion of historical debate highlights, 5 minutes 13 seconds on CBS, October 6; and a few seconds of an excerpt from the 1992 town hall debate on NBC, October 16. None of the post-debate specials immediately after the debates showed any excerpts from the debates themselves.[8]

There were significant differences in the way the networks treated the presidential debates. CBS devoted four lead or second stories to the debates; the other networks each had two lead or second stories focusing on the debates. CBS also made the greatest use of direct quotations from the debates, primarily in Erik Engberg's October 7 "Reality Check" of the claims made by the candidates. The networks were about equal in the number of times they treated the debates as a subordinate story within the general campaign story. CNN did so four times, and the other networks did so three times each.

In the post-debate specials, the most dramatic difference in coverage was CNN's decision to have Larry King interview minor party candidates rather than discuss the presidential debates. Meyrowitz has discussed the different "logics" used by media in deciding whom and what to cover. National media logic places great importance on the candidate's chance of winning the election, and relies heavily on party leaders and polls for information. By this logic, ABC, CBS, and NBC chose to discuss the debates of the two major party contenders. Public logic, in contrast, argues that all candidates should be covered. Larry King's focus on minor party candidates is an unusual instance of public logic being used by the national media.[9]

Campaign staff members did not speak on any of the post-debate specials. As Peter Jennings said, "We don't have spin-meisters (as we call them in the media) on to tell us exactly how well their man has done" (ABC, Oct. 6). However, the post-debate shows did interview running mates Al Gore and Jack Kemp, who spun their candidates into images of perfection.

Other notable differences in the post-debate specials were in network choices of outside experts, attention to the debate moderator's role, and discussion of the "quick polls" taken after the debates. CBS was the only network to invite a scholar on political debates, Dean Kathleen Hall Jamieson of the Annenberg School of Communication, to discuss the debates (Oct. 6 and 16, post-debate specials). Dean Jamieson provided a unique perspective, pointing out debate effects no one else was aware of, examining the accuracy of candidate claims, and discussing specific similarities and differences between the candidates' positions. CBS also invited Frank Rich, the drama critic of the *New York Times*, to discuss the debates from a theatrical perspective (Oct. 16, post-debate special). Only ABC drew on newspaper editors from major regional papers, the *Cleveland Plain Dealer*, *Miami Herald*, and *Denver Post*, to discuss how they would cover the debate for their readers (Oct. 6, post-debate special).

The only discussion of the role of the debate moderator, Jim Lehrer, occurred on ABC. Commentators Sam Donaldson and George Will remarked upon the way Lehrer posed the "character question" to President Clinton (Oct. 6). This discussion, though brief, made the point that the moderator had considerable power in the debate situation.

ABC and CBS made major use of "quick polls" on the response to the debates, and NBC polled a focus group watching the debate to see if any minds were changed (Oct. 6). Anchor Peter Jennings of ABC was the only person to raise questions about the wisdom of doing the "quick poll" after the debates. On both October 6 and 16, he spoke apologetically about the poll, referring to it as the "strange 'who won the debate' question" which was "almost the obligatory thing" after the debates (Oct. 6). "Not everybody likes this sort of thing," he reported (Oct. 16). Then he showed the poll results.

Hypothesis 4, that the debates would be described primarily in the words of the journalists, was supported. The anchors and reporters did most of the talking, introducing the topics of the debates, summarizing what the candidates were doing, quoting campaign staffers, and providing transitions from picture to picture. In the 31 different newscasts examined, in addition to the anchors, CBS used five reporters, NBC and ABC three reporters each, and CNN two reporters to discuss the debates. Two of the networks had their own analysts to discuss the debates: Jeff Greenfield for ABC, and Tim Russert for NBC.

While the networks' own people dominated the discussion, there was a second important group talking about the debates: the candidates themselves, their aides, and other prominent party members. In the 21 newscasts which mentioned the debates, the candidates were shown speaking about the debates in the following number of newscasts: Clinton, 10; Dole, 10; Perot, 3; Kemp, 2; Gore, 1. Eight Clinton aides were shown commenting on the debates. Joe Lockhart, the Clinton/Gore Press Secretary, was seen four times. A Democratic adviser from the 1984 campaign was also used. Three Dole aides were shown giving their "spin" on the debates, as well as two Republican advisers from past campaigns.

Two other kinds of debate discussants received little attention on the nightly news: the voters and experts. In only two newscasts, both the night after the first debate (Oct. 7), did voters speak about the debates. NBC News showed Lisa Myers discussing the debate with seven people from a focus group; ABC showed voters making short statements about the debates from four sections of the country. Voter opinions appeared mainly in the form of poll figures, or "numbered voices," as Susan Herbst has called them.[10] Seventeen of the thirty campaign stories cited poll results which measured the candidates' standing in the polls, as well as their performance in the debates.

In only one nightly newscast were experts interviewed. On October 6, CBS showed *60 Minutes* producer Don Hewitt, who had produced the Kennedy-Nixon debates, and Lawrence Grossman, former president of NBC News and author of *The Electronic Republic*, giving their insights on the debate. The post-debate specials made much more use of outside experts, including two university professors, the head of a political research firm, three newspaper editors from regional newspapers, a *Newsweek* editor, and a drama critic.

In their language discussing the debates, the networks generally characterized the events as "debates." However, there was one real maverick in the group. Anchor Dan Rather of CBS refused to use the term "debates." He usually used the term "joint appearance," but he also called them "odd political battles" (Oct. 6), a "controlled conversation" (Oct. 7), and a "happening in San Diego" (Oct. 17).

Another characteristic of network language was that debates were used as a kind of chronological and geographical marker, serving to organize the campaign news story. A typical example is Tom Brokaw's October 17 story on NBC: "In Presidential politics here at home tonight, after last night's debate in San Diego, both candidates were out on the stump trying to win California today." This highlighting and specificity is in sharp contrast to the coverage of the speeches in the primaries described by Kendall. She found that the networks gave little information about the location or audience of the speeches discussed, treating them almost generically, only briefly noting the date.[11] In the fall debates, all four networks actively touted the importance of the debates and the fact that they were carrying them live. They also seized upon the immediacy of the event and stressed their on-the-scene coverage.

Hypothesis 5 was that the networks would use debate excerpts chiefly as a form of proof to back up wider claims about the campaign. But the networks used so few debate excerpts that little analysis of this hypothesis was possible. The few examples supported the hypothesis. In the CBS October 7 "Reality Check," Erik Engberg showed debate excerpts and then stopped the tape to discuss the inaccuracies of the claims. The debate excerpts were proof of distortion. When historical debate excerpts were shown, they were used to illustrate what could go wrong in a debate, and how the town hall format had been a disadvantage to President Bush.

Although they made little use of debate excerpts, the networks clearly saw the debate as an important story. They treated the first debate as the news event itself, rather than giving it a subordinate role. The presidential debates were accorded the same independent news status as the State of the Union Address.[12] From a news perspective, the debates competed with other "big" stories, such as major sports events or terrible accidents. This was illustrated vividly when Peter Jennings interrupted the post-debate special on October 16 to announce two breaking news stories: the World Series score, and the report that there had been many deaths at a Guatemalan soccer match.

RESEARCH QUESTIONS

How Did the Media Present Clinton's Goals?

The networks treated President Clinton's goals only briefly, as though they were obvious: Clinton led in the polls before the debates, and thus he wanted to maintain his lead. As Rita Braver of CBS put it (Oct. 6): "For Bill Clinton the challenge tonight will be to strike exactly the right tone, and not to blow his lead with the voters." The New York Times imagery was similar: "In terms of campaign themes, Mr. Clinton is simply running out the clock."[13] After each debate, the Clinton campaign was said to be pleased, because the polls showed that the majority of viewers thought he had won the debate, and he had maintained his lead. Bracing for Dole's attacks in the second debate, Clinton adopted the goal and strategy of keeping to the high road, remaining presidential, and ignoring Dole's attacks. Afterwards, Rita Braver reported that his "campaign was elated," because he had followed through on this plan, and voters believed he had won (CBS, Oct. 17).

Clinton himself stated his goals in a different way, eschewing talk of winning or losing. "I want it to be essentially a positive thing," he said. "There will be obviously some clear contrasts between Senator Dole and me, but my belief is that people want us to try to talk about building a future, and that's what I'm going to try to do" (CNN, Oct. 5).

How Did the Media Present Dole's Goals?

The media devoted major attention to Senator Dole's debate goals, and set them exceedingly high. Nothing short of a huge change could be counted as success. Dole, in the underdog challenger role, had "the most to do," said Jeff Greenfield (ABC, Oct. 6, post-debate special). His goal was "to turn it around," said Tom Brokaw (NBC, Oct. 6, post-debate special). The night of the second debate, Brokaw described the event as "the last head-to-head chance for Bob Dole to catch up to President Clinton" (NBC, Oct. 16). "Hopes run high" in the Dole campaign of a major breakthrough, said Candy Crowley of CNN (Oct. 5). "This is the make or break for Bob Dole," said political analyst Kevin Phillips. "If he can do well here, he can get the ball rolling" (CBS, Oct. 6). He "needed a knock-out," said reporter Jim Miklaszewski of NBC (Oct. 7). Democratic strategist Tad Devine set the goal very high for Dole, not surprising for a partisan spinmeister: Dole needed to give such a "clear and convincing and compelling" performance that people planning to vote for Clinton would change their minds; he needed to "create a moment that will define the debate" and "dominate the coverage that follows" (CNN, Oct. 5).

Dole and his strategists were considerably more modest in

their publicly stated goals, putting on a spin which would reduce expectations. "I'll just do the best I can," said Dole. "I'll try to respond to the concerns that I think the audience has" (CBS, Oct. 6). Republican strategist David Keene said of the first debate: "His task is to make them comfortable with him in this debate" (CNN, Oct. 5). Dole did not agree with NBC reporter David Bloom that the second debate was an irrevocable benchmark, "his last chance to dramatically alter the course of the presidential race" (NBC, Oct. 16). According to Bloom, Dole wanted "to engage Clinton" on the character question. Dole aides thought he needed to be "very aggressive . . . on issues of presidential ethics and character" (NBC, Oct. 16).

How Did the Media Present the Rhetorical Strategies Used by Each Candidate in the Debate?

Much of the coverage of both candidates concerned this topic, with attention to the pre-debate strategies, the strategies in the debate itself, and the post-debate strategies. The networks alerted viewers to the fact that the campaigns were putting their own partisan slant on the debates, using the word "spin" frequently, as when NBC reporter Jim Miklaszewski announced that he was "standing in Spin Alley, where both sides are already dispensing their take on tonight's debate" (Oct. 16). The nightly news programs relied heavily on campaign "spinners" representing the candidates. Eric R. Appleman, an independent writer who covered the campaign, gave a vivid behind-the-scenes account of the spinning at the Hartford debate: "The thing that was most fascinating to me was the spin room scene. The spinners now have sign bearers accompanying them. Both the Republicans and Democrats had corners set up adjacent to spin alley, where the spinners could sit down and do satellite interviews with local stations. These are called media tours because the spinner goes through a whole series of stations."[14]

CLINTON'S RHETORICAL STRATEGIES

In pre-debate coverage, the networks discussed Clinton's use of several incumbent strategies identified with the institution of the presidency.[15] Rita Braver noted that he appeared in settings which made him look presidential, and working to convey a "dignified and presidential" manner (CBS, Oct. 6). Braver speculated that if Clinton showed any temper in the debate, it would be done deliberately, "to make Mr. Clinton look tough" (CBS, Oct. 6). CNN's Jill Dougherty reported that polls showed a "rally effect" for Clinton because of the Mideast talks he had held at the White House (Oct. 5). Clinton's efforts to convey a benign presidential image were discussed very specifically by CNN. Dougherty reported that Clinton was using a strategy of constructing "a Reaganesque message" just before the debate, running an ad in Reagan's 1984 "Morning in America" style. The ad stressed "taking care of the American people" (CNN, Oct. 5). Ann Lewis, Deputy Campaign Manager for Clinton, said that Clinton was also looking at some tapes of the Reagan 1984 campaign, which she said had been "just a brilliant example of the re-election of an incumbent" (CNN, Oct. 5).

Candidates often escalate attacks on their opponents just before the debates, to put them in a weakened condition and to lay the groundwork for attacks in the debates. Clinton did not do this personally. It would have been inconsistent with his "above the battle" strategy. However, the New York Times reported that the Clinton campaign spent "about $3 million . . . in the weeks leading up to the first Presidential debate to show a commercial attacking Mr. Dole's record across thirty years in office. The commercial was designed to drive down the Republican's poll numbers so he could not come out of the debate with a large advantage."[16] Clinton surrogates also dealt with Dole attacks and threats of attacks. When Dole gave a speech criticizing Clinton on foreign policy before the first debate, Clinton's press secretary Michael McCurry told ABC that if Dole made the same attack in the debate, Clinton would look him in the eye and recount his successes in Bosnia, North Korea, Haiti, and other countries (Oct. 3). Just before the second debate, Peter Knight, Clinton/Gore Campaign Manager, was shown saying that the town hall format of the debate was not "conducive to negative attacks." "I think the American people are sick of negative attacks," he said. NBC then showed the footage of the 1992 town hall debate in which an audience member asked, "Can we focus on the issues and not the personalities and the mud?" Reporter Jim Miklaszewski pointed out that this development had helped Clinton and hurt Bush, because the latter had planned to make negative attacks on Clinton (Oct. 16).

In the debate preparation period, Clinton and his aides were shown attempting to reduce expectations. He was preparing for the debate, but in a relaxed and unworried manner. On September 29, CNN reported that Clinton said he didn't have much time to prepare because of the Mideast summit. On October 6, Rita Braver cited Clinton press secretary Michael McCurry as saying that the President had played cards on the plane travelling to the debate, because he "wanted to do one thing he could win for sure" (CBS, Oct. 6). Pictures of Clinton in Chautauqua, New York in debate preparation mode showed him in casual clothes, smiling and talking with Senator George Mitchell, who was the stand-in for Bob Dole in the practice debates. Tom Brokaw joked about his claims that he was preparing strenuously, saying "the reality is a little less serious." The accompanying shot showed Clinton riding off to play golf (NBC, Oct. 4). CNN, too, showed a relaxed Clinton in Chautauqua, signing copies of his book and talking with people. "Hi kids," he said to some children (CNN, Oct. 5). According to reporter Jill Dougherty, Clinton aides said he was having trouble getting his answers down to the required 90 seconds, but was ready on the issues (CNN, Oct. 5).

In discussing the rhetorical strategies of the first debate itself, Jonathan Alter of *Newsweek* noted that Clinton had surpassed Dole in targeting women in the audience, because he had twice mentioned guaranteed hospital stays for women after they gave birth (ABC, Oct. 6). Phil Jones of CBS observed that Clinton had referred to Dole's tax cut plan five times as a "tax scheme," but Dole had not effectively answered the charge (Oct. 7). Jeff Greenfield of ABC praised Clinton as a "superb counterpuncher" (ABC, Oct. 6, post-debate special).

After the second debate, the networks gave attention to Clinton's conspicuous avoidance of a clash with Dole. Frank Rich, the drama critic of the *New York Times*, observed that while Clinton's refusal to answer Dole's aggressive questions had created a positive "above the fray" image, in a real debate Clinton would probably not have been allowed to avoid answering (Oct. 16, post-debate special). Brit Hume emphasized the strategic nature of Clinton's behavior; he had practiced for the debate with "relentless attack" from Senator George Mitchell, said Hume, and was "coached all the way not to respond to any of it" (ABC, Oct. 16, post-debate special). Hume gave the clear impression that this strategy had been a wise one. As a quick picture of the town hall participants appeared on the screen, he said, "And why should he [answer the attacks]? Those citizen-questioners showed no interest in such issues last night" (ABC, Oct. 17). Political expert Kevin Phillips wasn't so sure that Clinton had carried off this strategy successfully, however, saying that his worst moments in the debate were when he looked nervous on the moral questions (CBS, Oct. 16, post-debate special). Clinton himself was shown making statements the day after the debate defining his behavior in the above-the-battle mold: "We need not say bad things about our opponents to say we just have different views" (CBS, Oct. 17).

After both debates, the nightly news featured Clinton reiterating his positive, presidential, civics lesson theme about the value of debates and how much he had enjoyed participating. On ABC he was shown praising Senator Dole: "I thought it was a good debate. I thought he did well" (Oct. 7). He told CBS that "We just proved you can still do it [present different views] and be civilized and decent and humane . . . and that's the way we ought to conduct our public affairs in this country" (Oct. 7). On NBC, he was shown saying, "I enjoyed that debate," and remarking that people could see the differences in the two candidates. According to reporter Jim Miklaszewski, Clinton "celebrated with champagne well into the morning" (Oct. 7). After the second debate, CBS and ABC showed him extolling the value of keeping a civil tone when differing with one's opponent. He also praised the town hall questioners in a fatherly tone: "They did a fine job and they spoke for all of America and I was *very* proud of them, and I know you were too" (ABC, Oct. 17).

Immediately after the first debate, Peter Jennings received a memorandum from the Clinton campaign with their interpretation of the debate's results. Jennings held it up for viewers and remarked that the Clinton campaign, compared to the Dole campaign, was exceptionally well organized (ABC, Oct. 6).

The overall assessments of the quality of the debates followed a predictable pattern by partisans. For example, Vice President Gore said that Clinton "did an outstanding job" (NBC, Oct. 6, post-debate show).

In the hours and days immediately after the debates, the candidates and their surrogates were shown continuing the debate in their speeches and comments to the press. Even as he was interviewed about the first debate by the networks, Gore reiterated the campaign's agenda and the very language enunciated in the debate. "We've proposed tax cuts," he said, but they are "paid for" and "focused," while the Dole tax cuts would "blow a hole in the budget" (NBC, Oct. 6, post-debate special). When an organization of CEOs of Fortune 500 companies endorsed Clinton the day after the first debate, both Brit Hume of ABC and Jim Miklaszewski of NBC reported that this endorsement (which was shown on the screen) was being used by the Clinton campaign as a direct answer to a Dole charge in the debate that Clinton was a "liberal" (Oct. 7). Clinton was also shown personally answering another Dole debate charge, that Dole trusted the people while Clinton trusted the government. The question wasn't whether you trusted the government or the people, said Clinton, because "the government is just the people acting together" (NBC, Oct. 7).

Many of the network comments about Clinton related to his personal qualities, such as his above-the-battle manner, the ease with which he spoke to the town hall citizens, and his experience. Little was shown on the networks, except the debates themselves, that gave information about any of Clinton's policy positions.

DOLE'S RHETORICAL STRATEGIES

The media presented Dole as using two main pre-debate strategies: first, the typical challenger strategy of heightening attacks on the opponent, and second, attempting to diminish expectations about his debate performance. Like Clinton, Dole started a new ad just before the debates. It was "geared to framing the debate," and attacked Clinton for raising taxes, calling his policies "liberal."[17] Reporter Phil Jones of CBS said that the Dole campaign wanted to throw the President off stride on the question of ethics, and so they had invited Billy Dale, who had been fired as White House Travel Director by Clinton, to the first debate. The campaign attitude was "This is warfare," said Jones. As pictures appeared on the screen, he pointed out further evidence of this aggressiveness in the Dole supporters gathering outside the Bushnell Theatre in Hartford with signs attacking the Clinton scandals (Oct. 6).

The emphasis on Dole's attack strategy was heavier for the second debate, as he and his surrogates made many statements about how much tougher he was going to be. David Bloom of NBC reported that "top Dole aides say he must be very aggressive tonight on issues of presidential ethics and character" (Oct. 16). His campaign manager Scott Reed was shown saying about Clinton: "there's a pattern here of ethical lapses" (NBC, Oct. 16). But reporters noted that the town hall format, with 120 San Diego area residents asking questions, might well constrain Dole from attacking. This was especially so, said David Bloom of NBC, because Dole was "already trying to buck a reputation that he's mean-spirited" (Oct. 16).

Dole spent many days preparing for the first debate. The networks mentioned this preparation frequently, showing him sitting by the pool in Florida (CNN, Sept. 29; NBC, Oct. 4; CNN, Oct. 5). While the Dole campaign made it possible for the media to show Dole's preparations, they also used various techniques to show that he was relaxed. There was a certain tension in this double message that he was preparing with great care, but was very relaxed. Nelson Warfield, the campaign press secretary, tried to make the pieces fit: "It may look like he's just sitting beside the pool boiling like a lobster, but he's sitting there thinking like a fox. . . . There's a lot more going on than might be apparent."[18] He looked relaxed by the pool. He also clowned around a bit. In CNN footage on October 5, he was shown walking up the stairs with his wife, whereupon he suddenly tossed his manuscript into the air, as Candy Crowley said, "it seems that Bob Dole has had enough" (CNN, Oct. 5). In the same broadcast, when Dole was asked whether he was nervous, he grinned, shook his arm as though it was trembling, and asked, "Who me?" Dole and former President George Bush were shown discussing debate preparation by the pool. Dole said he had had enough, that it was "like filling up your tank with gas. It only holds so much." Bush agreed, and said that Dole was "all ready. He'll do well" (Oct. 5). Dole told his supporters that Clinton was such a good debater that "if I show up, I think I will win."[19] There was a playful aura to Dole's attitude toward the debates, as communicated by the media. The campaign's efforts to portray him as relaxed were successful; as CBS reporter Phil Jones said just before the first debate, Dole was "looking tanned, ready, and rested after nine hours of sleep" (Oct. 6). The accompanying footage of a smiling, vigorous Dole proved his claims. But the big investment of time in debate preparation was not forgotten by the reporters. When Dole made little gain in the polls after the debate, reporter Jim Wooten remarked on the disappointment of the Dole campaign, as they had "put a lot of eggs in the debate basket" (ABC, Oct. 7).

The networks were generally quite positive in their evaluations of Dole in the first debate. Jeff Greenfield portrayed him as a skilled debater, from long years in the Senate; after all, "the Senate is a debating institution" (ABC, Oct. 6, post-debate special). Tim Russert of NBC said he had "stayed on message" and taken steps to "assure his base" (Oct. 6, post-debate special). Tom Brokaw said that Dole had done "better than expected," and commented on the "entertaining" nature of the debate (NBC, Oct. 6, post-debate special). NBC examined the evidence from the Dialathon used by their focus group audience and spoke with them to see where the strengths and weaknesses were. It was clear that the audience had enjoyed Dole's humor, that they had not liked his chiding of Clinton about the need to be respectful and address the president as "Mr. President," and they had not liked his conclusion telling young people not to use drugs. But the information was presented so quickly, and with so little explanation, that the nature and significance of the report was unclear (Oct. 6, post-debate special). Jonathan Alter, *Newsweek* columnist, thought Clinton much more effective than Dole with women watching the debate. Dole had missed his target audience of soccer moms, said Alter (ABC, Oct. 6, post-debate special).

The ABC commentators were harder on Dole's rhetoric in the second debate. One criticism was of his failure to develop his attack. Sam Donaldson said that Dole "jabbed a little bit," but failed to press the character issue. Donaldson claimed that, to be effective, Dole needed to make a "sustained barrage" over a period of months (ABC, Oct. 16, post-debate special). George Will said Dole's explanations were "garbled," as, for example, when he failed to make a distinction between affirmative action and racial preferences (Oct. 16, post-debate special). Jeff Greenfield, however, thought it "a fine performance for Senator Dole," who seemed comfortable with the format. It was like being in the well of the Senate, said Greenfield (Oct. 16, post-debate special).

CBS was more positive. Rita Braver began by saying that she thought that "Bob Dole got to the President a little bit." Bob Schieffer and Kevin Phillips agreed that Dole had done better in the second debate than the first. Dole was "sharper," said Schieffer. He also admired his humor, mentioning the Dole line, "If I were a senior citizen . . ." (Oct. 16, post-debate special). Phillips thought Dole was best when he emphasized moral issues and why people should trust him, though he was weak when he lapsed into "Dolespeak" (Oct. 16, post-debate special).

Many of the comments about Dole on the networks related to his personal qualities, such as his sense of humor, age, credibility, and characteristics as a speaker. However, there was little network attention to where Dole stood on the issues in the debate, or on the accuracy of his arguments and proofs.

Clearly the Dole campaign's rhetorical strategy after the debates was to stress victory. Of the first debate, Elizabeth Dole said, "Bob Dole won" (NBC, Oct. 6, post-debate special). Running mate Kemp exalted, "Bob Dole stole the night" (ABC, Oct. 6, post-debate special). Dole's campaign manager, Scott Reed, dismissed the overnight polls, which showed little gain, as "meaningless," and pointed to the enthusiastic crowds in New Jersey. They were a "direct reflection of last night," he said (ABC, Oct. 7). Network coverage after the second debate was substantially lighter, however, and as none of Dole's surrogates were interviewed, no claims of victory were heard.

Post-debate coverage of Dole and his surrogates showed them carrying on with the debate themes. Jack Kemp contrasted Dole with Clinton: Dole "trusted the people," said Kemp, while Clinton "trusted the government" (CBS, Oct. 6, post-debate special). The day after the debate, ABC and CNN showed Dole discussing his attack strategy. "We're going to get tough in this campaign," he said. "You haven't seen anything yet. Last night was a warm-up" (Oct. 17). CBS showed him complaining about Clinton's avoidance of clash: "We couldn't engage the President. He didn't want to talk about the issues" (Oct. 17). Reporters made the link between the debates and Dole's subsequent statements. Brit Hume of ABC said that the day after the second debate, Dole had challenged Clinton on the pardons again, and said that Clinton wouldn't answer (Oct. 17). Linden Soles of CNN also made the tie: "On the day after their second and more aggressive debate, Bill Clinton and Bob Dole are continuing to trade rhetorical fire." Their remarks, he said, "had echoes from last night" (Oct. 17).

COVERAGE OF ARGUMENTS AND EVIDENCE

There was little attention in this network coverage to the nature and quality of the arguments and evidence used in the debates. The main exceptions were the CBS post-debate specials on October 6 and October 16, and the CBS nightly news of October 7. On both October 6 and 16, CBS had Kathleen Hall Jamieson, Dean of the Annenberg School of Communication, as an expert commentator. While other commentators repeatedly asserted that there was nothing new in the debate, she pointed out that the debates had accomplished several important things. They had made clear to the viewers the major differences between the candidates on the "role of government," on such matters as the Family and Medical Leave Act, for example. She stressed the importance of the "common dimensions" which the debate had revealed, such as the agreement of the candidates on some basic ground concerning IRAs, the capital gains tax, and most important, the commission to solve the Medicare shortfall (CBS, Oct. 16, post-debate special). She discussed the deceptive way Clinton had discussed Dole's position on Medicare, and the deceptive way Dole had discussed Clinton's tax increases. There had been some clarification on both issues in the debate that night, she said (CBS, Oct. 16, post-debate special). Her comments were unique in informing the viewer of the different positions of the candidates, as well as dissecting the accuracy of candidate claims. She focused on the invention of the speakers as they constructed their arguments, and the importance of knowing about that, rather than whether the debate had "turned the campaign around."

Erik Engberg's "Reality Check" of the first debate was the only other major analysis of the substance of a debate in the network coverage examined. One by one, he showed specific candidate statements from the first debate, and then called "Time Out," telling the audience how inaccurate and deceptive the claim was. Clinton had said that he would try to "make this campaign and this debate one of ideas, not insults," but Engberg said that 94 percent of Clinton's ads were negative. Dole said he wouldn't comment on certain topics, all the while talking about them in the debate: "And I won't comment on other things that have happened in your administration or your past about drugs." Dole had spent 11 seconds misinforming the viewer about the cost of taxes under the Clinton administration, said Engberg. Clinton had attacked Dole's budget for cutting Medicare $270 billion, but Engberg showed that the Republican budget proposal slowed the growth of Medicare rather than cut it. As with Jamieson's critique, Engberg was very specific and informative, focusing on the arguments and proofs of the candidates, and backing up his evaluation with concrete evidence directly from the debate (CBS, Oct. 7).

Peter Jennings of ABC also briefly raised the topic of debate accuracy in his post-debate remarks, advising the audience to look for the "truth squads" on morning television, newspapers, and radio (ABC, Oct. 6, post-debate special). CNN gave Ross Perot a long 42 seconds to attack the content and quality of the first debate. He argued that the debate would have been much better had he not been excluded. He lambasted the candidates for failing to discuss corrupt campaign practices, and briefly developed arguments for reforms in the campaign schedule, finances, and time of voting (Oct. 7).

The network anchors made general assessments of the quality of the debates the instant the candidates stopped speaking, their voices competing for viewer attention with the swirl of activity on the stage as the candidates hugged and shook hands with their families and friends. These sweeping judgments were all positive: the candidates had done well, the presentations were strong, the atmosphere was civilized, said the anchors.

EFFECTS OF THE DEBATE

Trent and Friedenberg present eight possible effects of presidential debates.[20] Only one of those effects—shifting limited numbers of voters—received much attention in network discussion of the 1996 debates. Overwhelmingly, the reporters and experts claimed that there was little effect, little change produced by the debates, because the voters had not shifted their support from one candidate to the other. Professor Nelson Polsby of the University of California at Berkeley, an expert for ABC, said that people had made their minds up before the debate, and thus, the debate "was a wash" (Oct. 16, post-debate special). Tom Brokaw, citing polls and groups of representative voters, said that the debate "did not cause any seismic shifts in voter support" (NBC, Oct. 7). Jeff Greenfield and Sam Donaldson of ABC expected no change would result from the debate (Oct. 16). All the post-debate programs used polls to show that Clinton had won both debates, Dole had lost, and there had been no major change in voter preferences. Even Peter Jennings of ABC, who did express some discomfiture about the "quick polls," followed the pack. "After last night's debate," he reported, "President Clinton still holds a commanding lead over Bob Dole" (ABC, Oct. 17). Debate effects were reported mainly as an extension of the poll reports. Dole had not scored the "knock-out punch" he needed, reported Bob Schieffer (CBS, Oct. 16). At most, Tim Russert of NBC ventured, Dole might "get a small pop" from the first debate (Oct. 6, post-debate special). George Will said Dole had helped his base, whereas he had had "no pulse" before the debate (ABC, Oct. 6, post-debate special).

This narrow focus on shifting voter preferences ignored the fact that many other effects were also possible: increasing audience size, reinforcing audiences, helping to set voters' agendas, increasing voters' knowledge of issues, modifying candidate images, freezing the campaign, and building confidence in U.S. democracy.[21] Audience size did receive attention. But the networks focused on the drop in viewership from 1992 (NBC, ABC, CBS, Oct. 7). The fact that about 70 million people watched the first debate, an extraordinarily large national audience for any event, received no real notice.

Newspeople and others touched lightly on some effects besides voter change. Political analyst Kevin Phillips noted that if there was no change after the debates, Clinton would gain more than Dole, because the campaign would begin "to freeze" (CBS, Oct. 6, post-debate special). Dan Rather thought the debates were important to Dole because they introduced him to lots of people (CBS, Oct. 6, post-debate special). Political analyst Cokie Roberts thought that people seeing the candidates for the first time would learn something from the debates (ABC, Oct. 6, postdebate special). But only Kathleen Hall Jamieson discussed the many and complex possible effects of the presidential debates (CBS, Oct. 6, post-debate special).

DISCUSSION AND CONCLUSIONS

There are four main findings from this study of media coverage of the 1996 presidential debates. First, the networks gave the debates major coverage by any standard. Second, by discussing the debate effects almost entirely in terms of whether they produced a big change in the campaign, they created an impossible hurdle for Senator Dole, while disregarding basic principles of persuasion and campaign communication. Third, the networks gave little consideration to the power of the moderator. Fourth, as with coverage of previous presidential debates, the networks focused on the candidates' images rather than their ideas.

The networks gave the debates major coverage by any standard. Each network showed the debates in their entirety, as well as devoting a follow-up program of substantial length to discussion of the debates. In the nightly newscasts in the September 29–October 23, 1996 period studied, 68 percent of the newscasts discussed the debates, and 39 percent of the lead stories contained mention of the debates.[22] This was particularly true for the first debate. Unlike Kendall's findings about presidential primary campaign speeches, the debates were treated as specific news events in themselves, with much emphasis on where and when they were held. The presidential debates, like the State of the Union message, occupy a place on the short list of American speeches accorded the status of a lead story on network television news.[23]

While according the debates a major place in the news, the networks so constructed the discussion of the debate effects as to create an impossible hurdle for Senator Dole, the challenger and underdog in the campaign. Debate effects were weighed chiefly in terms of whether they produced a big change in the campaign. This approach disregarded basic principles of persuasion and campaign communication.

"Any surprises?" asked Dan Rather of his reporters and other analysts again and again after the first and second debates (CBS, Oct. 6 and 16, post-debate show). "Any change?" asked Tom Brokaw of the voters in the focus group after the first debate (NBC, Oct. 6, post-debate show). The words "surprise" and "change" imply noticeable change, startling change, the kind that would make a good news story. They are consistent with a long-rejected view of persuasion, the "hypodermic needle" model, which assumes that a single persuasive message will produce immediate change in the receiver, just as a single shot from a hypodermic needle can do. But political campaigns involve the presentation of multiple messages over time, in a sustained effort to influence the voters, whether by shaping, reinforcing, or changing their views. The expectation that a single message will produce instantaneous change is naive and outdated. Evidence of effects from the presidential debates through history shows not a single example of a presidential debate producing a major turnaround in public opinion.

How, then, did this criterion of immediate change become the focus for evaluation of the presidential debates? There are several possible explanations. Some people undoubtedly suspect that the networks were displaying a pro-Clinton bias. More Clinton partisans than Dole partisans were interviewed in these programs, and in one instance, news anchor Peter Jennings said that the Clinton campaign was better organized than the Dole campaign (ABC, Oct. 6). The whole perspective of setting the goal so high for Dole, suggesting that he must be so effective in the debates that he would succeed in catching up with Clinton, put Dole at a real disadvantage, and was consistent with the spinning being done by the Clinton surrogates.

However, there are other possible explanations for the networks' narrow criteria. One comes from the nature of debate itself. Dole was the challenger, the one advocating a change from the *status quo*. Dole was in effect the affirmative debater who has a burden of proof to show that there should be a change from the *status quo*. In portraying Clinton's need to "hold his own" in the debates and Dole's need to produce a major change, the networks were consistent with the traditional criteria for evaluating debates. There is some support for this explanation in the fact that the networks paid much more attention before the debate to Dole's goals than to Clinton's. As Jeff Greenfield said, Dole had "the most to do" (ABC, Oct. 6, post-debate special). To verify this analysis, researchers need to look at media coverage of underdogs/challengers in other presidential debates.

Another possible explanation for the adoption of this narrow effects criterion is that the networks followed the national media logic described by Meyrowitz, to the exclusion of other approaches.[24] By this logic, reporters for the national media rely almost exclusively upon polls and national party leaders for their news agenda, in contrast to local media logic and public logic. Jack Germond, of the *Baltimore Sun*, supported this explanation, saying "Dole arrived at the debate with the consensus in the political community and his own party that he needed to change the dynamics of the campaign radically to have any chance of overtaking Clinton, who leads in most national polls by 12 to 15 points."[25] In the newscasts examined, the voices speaking most frequently were journalists, and second, candidates and their staffs. Seldom were outside experts or members of the public interviewed. These findings are consistent with Meyrowitz's analysis. Heavy reliance on polls and party insiders is also characteristic of "pack journalism." Reporters travel with the candidates, and talk mainly with each other and with the candidates and their staffs, in a kind of cocoon. They add poll results to their stories, as a way of providing some representation of the voters' voice.

Finally, one could argue that the networks set up a "must win" scenario because that was the most exciting, the most consistent with their role as an entertainment medium, and would improve their ratings the most. The horse race approach typical of debate coverage in the past proved true in 1996 as well. The drama of a race is in winning and losing. By setting up the debates as a win-lose horse race, the networks could build up the drama. There is evidence for this explanation in the timing and amount of their coverage. The heaviest attention to the debates occurred for the first debate. Once it became clear that the viewership was down, a fact mentioned by three of the four networks the night after the debate, the emphasis on debate stories fell precipitously. The drop in debate viewership also became part of the story of the electorate's lack of interest in the campaign.

A peculiar omission in network coverage of the debates was their failure to consider the role of the moderator. In both the first presidential debate and the vice presidential debate, one moderator, Jim Lehrer of PBS, asked all the questions. The agenda-setting power of his position was unmistakable. Yet in discussing the debates, reporters focused almost exclusively on the two presidential candidates, as though they had full command of the dialogue. In only one program, the post-debate special on ABC on October 6, did George Will and Sam Donaldson note the moderator's power. The kind of critique made by Walter Shapiro in *USA Today* never emerged on the networks. Shapiro charged that while Lehrer's questions were fair, they were so bland, and presented in such a colorless, flat tone that they "drain[ed] the energy out of the room," and reduced public interest. He also faulted Lehrer for neglecting to raise ethical questions, especially on political fund-raising.[26] One could argue that the candidates had the freedom to say whatever they wanted to say, and point to the many occasions when they ignored Lehrer's questions at least briefly while they developed their own agendas. But still, there were *three* active parties in the debates, not two, and one of those, the moderator, went virtually unmentioned in the network evaluations. No one examined the content or style of his questions. Instead, the responsibility for the success or failure of the debates was made to fall entirely on the two candidates.

Network coverage focused much more heavily on the candidates' personal qualities than on their ideas, a finding consistent with those of past research studies. For those viewers just tuning in to the campaign, information on the candidates' character (such as competence, empathy, strength, honesty) is valuable in forming judgments, and "plays a more decisive role than issues."[27] Television's debate coverage served these needs well. As Schroeder has pointed out, "the cult of personality . . . permeates television," and "for viewers, presidential candidates function as glorified television characters."[28] But near the end of the presidential campaign, many voters wanted more, seeking information on the candidates' positions. Those who had not watched the debates found little such information in the network coverage.

That the networks gave three hours each (90 minutes for each of two debates) to show the 1996 presidential debates was a positive contribution. Those who watch debates generally say they find them to be valuable. But the network construction of the story as though the success or failure of Senator Dole rested on the debates was a narrow and flawed perspective. Future debate coverage needs to recognize the many possible effects of debates as messages within a wider campaign and culture, and their important role in shaping and reinforcing opinion, not just in producing a dramatic change.

NOTES

1. The author wishes to thank John Tedesco for his comments on an earlier draft, and Jeremy Hinck for his assistance with videotaping. I am also grateful to my graduate students at the University at Albany, State University of New York, Fall 1996, for their insights on this topic.

2. These studies are summarized in Susan A. Hellweg, Michael Pfau, and Steven R. Brydon, *Televised Presidential Debates* (New York: Praeger, 1992), pp. 98–99. Also see James B. Lemert, William R. Elliott, William L. Rosenberg, and James M. Bernstein, *The Politics of Disenchantment: Bush, Clinton, Perot and the Press* (Cresskill, N.J.: Hampton Press, 1996).

3. See Hellweg, Pfau, and Brydon, *Televised Presidential Debates;* Lemert, Elliott, Rosenberg, and Bernstein, *The Politics of Disenchantment;* Diana Owen, "The Debate Challenge: Candidate Strategies in the New Media Age," in *Presidential Campaign Discourse: Strategic Communication Problems,* ed. Kathleen E. Kendall (Albany: State University of New York Press, 1995), pp. 135–155; Tom Rosenstiel, *Strange Bedfellows: How Television and the Presidential Candidates Changed American Politics, 1992* (New York: Hyperion, 1993), pp. 317–323; Alan Schroeder, "Watching Between the Lines: Presidential Debates as Television," *Press/Politics* 1 (Fall 1996): 57–75.

4. Kathleen E. Kendall, "Public Speaking in the Presidential Primaries Through Media Eyes," *American Behavioral Scientist* 37 (November 1993): 240–251.

5. Ibid.

6. Ibid.

7. Ibid.

8. According to "Dole Campaign in Discord," *New York Times,* October 11, 1996, p. A30, Dole's remarks about "Democrat wars" from the 1976 debate were "repeatedly played in the weeks leading to the first debate." However, this excerpt did not appear in the news programs examined here.

9. Joshua Meyrowitz, "The Problem of Getting on the Media Agenda: A Case Study in Competing Logics of Campaign Coverage," in *Presidential Campaign Discourse: Strategic Communication Problems,* ed. Kathleen E. Kendall (Albany: State University of New York Press, 1995), pp. 35–67.

10. Susan Herbst, *How Opinion Polling Has Shaped American Politics* (Chicago: University of Chicago Press, 1993).

11. Kendall, "Public Speaking in the Presidential Primaries Through Media Eyes," p. 243.

12. Ibid.

13. Allison Mitchell, "Clinton Campaign Finds Harmony After a Swift Exit by Morris," *New York Times,* October 15, 1996, p. A25.

14. Eric Appleman, personal correspondence to author, January 2, 1997.

15. Jimmie D. Trent and Judith S. Trent, "The Incumbent and His Challengers: The Problem of Adapting to Prevailing Conditions," in *Presidential Campaign Discourse: Strategic Communication Problems,* ed. Kathleen E. Kendall (Albany: State University of New York Press, 1995), pp. 69–92.

16. Mitchell, "Clinton Campaign Finds Harmony," p. A25.

17. Adam Nagourney, "Clinton and Dole Study For Debate and Swap Punches," *New York Times,* October 4, 1996, p. A1.

18. Katharine Q. Seelye, "As Dole Sits by Pool in Florida, He May Look Relaxed, But His Aides Say He's Working Hard," *New York Times*, September 29, 1996, p. A22.

19. Stewart Powell and Vic Ostrowidski, "Both Parties Put Spin on Debates," Albany *Times Union*, October 3, 1996, p. A-3.

20. Judith S. Trent and Robert V. Friedenberg, *Political Campaign Communication: Principles and Practices*, 3rd ed. (Westport, Conn.: Praeger, 1995).

21. Ibid.

22. These figures are skewed on the high side because they include the newscasts on all four networks the night after each debate.

23. Kendall, "Public Speaking in the Presidential Primaries Through Media Eyes," p. 243.

24. Meyrowitz, "The Problem of Getting on the Media Agenda."

25. Jack Germond, "Dole's Last Stand Doesn't Live Up To Its Advance Billing," *Baltimore Sun*, in Albany *Times Union*, October 17, 1996, p. A-6.

26. Walter Shapiro, "'With All Due Respect,' These Debates Are Dull," *USA Today*, October 11–13, 1996, p. 4A.

27. Hellweg et. al., *Televised Presidential Debates*, p. 109.

28. Schroeder, "Watching Between the Lines," p. 59.

SELECT BIBLIOGRAPHY

Note: Since this chapter was written immediately after the debates, little substantive work on the debates had yet been published. The author's main sources were: *ABC World News Tonight*, *CBS Evening News*, *CNN Prime News*, and *NBC Nightly News*, for the period from September 29 through October 23, 1996.

The following sources were also valuable.

Kendall, Kathleen E. "Public Speaking in the Presidential Primaries Through Media Eyes." *American Behavioral Scientist* 37 (November/December 1993): 240–251. Kendall studies network news coverage of the speeches and debates in the 1992 presidential primary campaign and argues that the candidates' words were replaced almost completely by journalistic descriptions, with speeches reduced to pictures of the candidates' delivery.

Owen, Diana. "The Debate Challenge: Candidate Strategies in the New Media Age." In *Presidential Campaign Discourse: Strategic Communication Problems*, ed. Kathleen E. Kendall (Albany: State University of New York Press, 1995), pp. 135–155. The author provides a useful overview of presidential debates, with attention to media coverage and the phases of the debate process. Her analysis focuses on the 1992 presidential debates.

Schroeder, Alan. "Watching Between the Lines: Presidential Debates as Television." *Press/Politics* 1 (Fall 1996): 57–75. Schroeder compares presidential debates to other high-profile television programs which are personality driven, promote conflict, and have real potential for risk because they are broadcast live. He compares the demands on debate performance of Old Television and New Television, providing many examples.

Trent, Judith S., and Robert V. Friedenberg. *Political Campaign Communication: Principles and Practices*, 3rd ed. (Westport, Conn.: Praeger, 1995). Chapter 8, pp. 228–236, is especially useful in its consideration of the effects of presidential debates.

Debate Transcripts

The author referred to the transcripts of the first and second presidential debates, obtained through the home page of the Commission on Presidential Debates (www.debates96.org). "The First 1996 Presidential Debate: Hartford, CT," transcript from the Commission on Presidential Debates. "Presidential Debate: San Diego, CA, October 16, 1996," transcribed from the Commission on Presidential Debates.

Chapter 2

The 1996 Gore-Kemp Vice Presidential Debates

Gaut Ragsdale

On October 9, 1996, at Bayfront Center's Mahaffey Theater in St. Petersburg, Florida, Republican Jack Kemp told those listening to a vice presidential debate between him and Vice President Albert Gore that his party's economic policies were not "trickle down" but like "Niagara Falls."[1] Kemp's waterfall metaphor was a striking contrast to the pejorative trickle-down metaphor that Democrats had long used to criticize Republican economic policies. For Kemp, Niagara Falls functioned as a positive image to talk about the economic policies that he was advocating. Vice President Gore, however, was unwilling to let Kemp completely recast the water metaphor. He focused Kemp's metaphor on the negative by saying Kemp and his presidential running mate Robert Dole would "put the economy in a barrel and send it over the falls." The interaction between these two vice presidential nominees over this water metaphor reveals a lot about this debate. Kemp, the positive and energetic challenger, was eager to talk about his economic policies, while Gore, the incumbent, was content to focus on winning by defending the Clinton administration and attacking the legitimacy of the Republican ticket.

The debate between Gore and Kemp also offered a contrast

between the 1992 and the 1996 vice presidential debates. The 1992 debate was unique because of three candidates in the race, the closeness of the election, and the confrontations between two of the three candidates—Gore and Quayle. The 1996 debate had only two participants, and it was marked by civility between the candidates rather than clashes. At the time of this debate, the Clinton/Gore ticket had a double-digit lead in the polls. Moreover, television viewership of the 1996 vice presidential debate was down compared to the previous vice presidential debate. In 1996, an estimated 26 million homes watched the debate compared to over 51 million in 1992.[2] Hence, while the 1992 debate was unique, the 1996 debate could be characterized as being a "routine" part of the presidential campaign.

The 1996 vice presidential debate was the second of three debates. Bob Dole was criticized after the first debate on October 6, 1996, for not attacking Clinton on issues and behaviors linked to his personal life. There was speculation after that debate whether or not Kemp would fulfill the traditional role of challenger in the vice presidential debate and attack the incumbent president and his administration. The vice presidential debate was held on October 9, 1996, and the Clinton/Gore campaign held approximately a 20-point lead in the polls before and after this event.[3] The final debate was held on October 16, 1996, one week after the vice presidential debate. What follows reveals the extent to which the 1996 vice presidential debate was an institutionalized part of the national campaign and how each candidate employed message strategies to perform effectively in the debate.

PRE-DEBATE STRATEGIES

The pre-debate strategies followed by the vice presidential candidates encompassed routine strategies associated with this phase of national political campaign debates. Vice President Gore prepared by arriving in St. Petersburg, Florida on the Saturday before the Wednesday evening debate. He practiced with former House of Representatives member Thomas J. Downey (D-NY). Gore and Downey engaged in four ninety-minute debates, in preparation for the event. Jack Kemp suspended active campaigning on Sunday, October 6, 1996, and traveled to Bal Harbour, Florida to prepare for the debate. Kemp used the same practice site that Bob Dole used to prepare for the presidential debate with Bill Clinton. Unlike Gore, Kemp had never debated one-to-one on national television. In preparing for the event, he engaged in three dress rehearsals which modeled the debate's format. Kemp's three mock debates were taped on closed-circuit television. He received feedback on his performance from aides who watched the tapes. The video tapes were used to provide Kemp with feedback related to his delivery and the length of his answers. Senator Judd Gregg, a Republican from New Hampshire, played the role of Gore during Kemp's practice sessions. In practicing, both candidates worked on generating answers that would fit into 90 seconds for initial questions, 60-second answers for rebuttal, and 30-second answers for follow-up responses to rebuttals. The format also included a closing statement lasting up to three minutes for each candidate. It was agreed upon during the debate negotiations that there would be no opening statements for the vice presidential debate. Except for the omission of the opening statement, this was the same format used in the first debate between Bob Dole and Bill Clinton. This format was a challenge for Kemp, who was known for providing lengthy and wandering answers to questions.[4] Kemp acknowledged this in his response to the moderator's first question of the debate. In asking this question the moderator, Jim Lehrer, reminded the candidates of the time limits. Kemp replied: "Wow, in 90 seconds? I can't clear my throat in 90 seconds."

Both candidates prepared by advancing and defending their major campaign themes, and questioning and taking issue with those themes and policies of the opposition. Gore was particularly thorough in preparing, and a good example of this was his response to Kemp's Niagara Falls metaphor. Gore's response "was totally canned."[5] Gore's campaign team had learned that Kemp liked to use the waterfall metaphor in his speeches, and the vice president was ready to ridicule it if Kemp used it in the debate. Gore was also ready to respond to another favorite Kemp metaphor: "to grow the pie." Kemp frequently used this metaphor to make reference to expanding and extending the national economy to all Americans. Had Kemp used the pie metaphor, which he did not, Gore was prepared to say: "The problem with your scheme to grow the pie is that it's full of half-baked ideas that will leave the American people with crumbs."[6] Gore's attention to frequently used metaphors by Kemp provides insight into the comprehensiveness of his preparation and helps account for the thoroughness and coherence of his answers. Thus, Gore and Kemp engaged in standard pre-debate preparation strategies by studying the issues, generating answers, and orally rehearsing for the debate.

During this phase, both Gore and Kemp also sought to lower expectations of their own individual performance while raising them for the opponent. Andrew Cuomo, who assisted Gore with debate preparations, noted that Kemp was an accomplished speaker who had earned nearly two million dollars in speaking fees in the two years prior to the fall presidential campaign.[7] The Kemp campaign noted that Kemp had never debated in a national, one-on-one, political debate and that Gore had gained such experience in the 1988 presidential race and again in 1993 when the vice president debated Ross Perot about United States Senate ratification of the North American Free Trade Agreement (NAFTA).[8] This was a televised debate between Gore and Perot on the *Larry King Live* show broadcast on CNN on November 9, 1993. Thus, both candidates sought to meet the expectations associated with pre-debate strategies. The greater burden was on challenger Kemp and his advisers due to his lack of debate experience at this level of politics. Although he had debated in 1988 when he was a candidate for the presidential nomination of the Republican party, those debates were state- or region-wide and involved multiple candidates and often multiple moderators. In terms of format and significance of outcomes, primary debates are simply not the same as debates occurring during a national political campaign.

The vice presidential debate was moderated by Jim Lehrer of PBS's *Newshour*. Lehrer had served as moderator of the third debate in 1992. This debate was divided by Lehrer serving as the single moderator during the first half of the debate. During the second half he was joined by three other panelists. After this 1992 debate the single moderator debate was praised and Mr.

Lehrer was highly praised for his effectiveness as a moderator.[9] In 1996, Lehrer served as moderator for all three debates. During the vice presidential debate he asked 23 questions. Most of these were primary questions dealing with single topics such as the following: "What measurement do you use, Mr. Kemp, in saying the economy is not growing the way it should be?" In many instances, Lehrer's questions would develop a complex topic. A question about Affirmative Action prompted specific questions about race in America and government policies for the country's inner cities. Near the end of the debate foreign policy was addressed in a series of questions, one each about Bosnia, Haiti, and Mexico. Lehrer also raised questions that probed candidate answers such as the following: "Mr. Vice President, what about Mr. Kemp's point that he's made a couple of times that what we need is to throw away the current—the present tax code and write a whole new tax system. Do you agree with that?" At another point Lehrer probed Kemp's answer: "Mr. Kemp, back to the philosophy question. Do you think there's a basic philosophy difference between these two tickets, or is it about specifics, which both of you have talked about?" Lehrer's ability to ask primary questions, develop a line of questions, and employ probing, follow-up questions enabled him to overcome many of the criticisms associated with prior debates where panelists were prone to ask lengthy, multiquestions often without opportunities to probe or follow up on candidate answers.[10] Also, Lehrer's questions elicited more than information. As the previous questions reveal, they prompted a discussion of differences between the two candidates and their running mates. Two questions in particular reveal focus on more than just obtaining information: "Mr. Kemp, Senator Dole has criticized the president on Haiti, that he handled it wrong. What did he do wrong?" And, "Mr. Vice President, should federal government Affirmative Action programs be continued?"

The major omission in Lehrer's questions for the vice presidential debate was specific consideration of how each candidate would fulfill the role of vice president if elected. The questions were not specific to the vice presidency. They were just as fitting to the presidential candidates as they were to Gore and Kemp. Carlin and Bicak have argued that questions about the vice presidency and related functions and expectations are important, especially if there are differences between candidates on the same ticket.[11] This point applies to Kemp because, after 90 minutes of the debate, listeners were aware that there were policy differences between Kemp and Dole, yet they did not know what role Kemp would play in a Dole administration. Likewise, audience members had no indication of how Vice President Gore's role would change, if at all, if reelected.

CANDIDATE GOALS

As the incumbent vice president, Gore pursued two primary issue goals. The first was to defend and promote the Clinton administration's record by arguing the administration had benefitted American voters, especially middle-income voters. By appealing to middle-income voters he was also able to appeal to many undecided and independent voters, especially independents who had voted for Ross Perot in 1992. A second goal was to attack the policy proposals and the candidates comprising the Republican ticket. In addition to these goals the vice president sought three interrelated goals: articulating and repeating a memorable theme, linking specific issues to middle-income voters, and debating not to lose. The pursuit of these three goals would enable the Clinton/Gore ticket to accomplish its two primary issue goals. The image goals of the vice president were expected: bolster the image of the Clinton administration as well as the vice president and negatively modify the image of the Dole/Kemp ticket.

As challenger, Jack Kemp sought three primary goals. The first dealt with diminishing the accomplishments and record of the Clinton administration. Kemp also sought to appeal to his Republican base and reach out to undecided and independent voters. A related goal for Kemp was to appeal to minority voters and voters living in the inner city—voters often associated with the Democratic party. This goal was more candidate-specific than party-specific. Kemp had long been a champion of civil rights and capitalism.[12] He believed that capitalism was an effective means to improve civil rights and economic conditions for all Americans. Linked to this was Kemp's belief that high taxes prevented capitalism from flourishing and therefore should be reduced substantially.[13] Kemp also pursued the goals linking issues to specific voting groups and debating not to lose. He also advocated a major theme (vaguely) about cutting taxes throughout the debate. Kemp's image goals were also expected and critical to him as the Republican challenger. As the lesser known of the two candidates, it was important for Kemp to be perceived as possessing presidential leadership qualities, and being worthy of being on the national ticket. Clearly this was the dominant image goal for Kemp. A secondary goal was to diminish the image of the Clinton administration.

ISSUE DEVELOPMENT

In developing issue goals, both candidates relied on accepted strategies used in prior national campaign debates. The issue goal of developing an overall theme was prominent and both men used accepted strategies for developing this goal. One strategy is to include the overall theme in opening and closing statements. Another is to integrate the theme into as many answers as possible. Gore excelled in repeating major themes in different answers. His overall theme was: "We have a plan to balance the budget while protecting Medicare, Medicaid, education, and the environment." This theme was uttered during Gore's initial answer which was a 60-second response to Kemp's first answer. In what should have been a 60-second rebuttal to Kemp's answer about Bob Dole's unwillingness to talk about personal and ethical differences between himself and Clinton, Gore answered with a clear reference to the dominant theme of the Clinton/Gore campaign. In the Clinton campaign this theme was referred to as M2E2, or Medicare, Medicaid, education, and the environment.[14] Hence, even though there was no official opening statement, Vice President Gore made sure that the campaign theme was included in his initial remarks of the evening. In effect Gore transformed a rebuttal answer into an opening speech.

The second time he spoke Gore was asked about the different political philosophies between him and Kemp, and again he repeated the dominant campaign theme for the Democratic ticket. In this answer, he indicated that he was offering a positive plan based on three principles—opportunity for all Americans, responsibility being accepted by everyone, and strengthening communities. He concluded this second response by saying: "All of this is within a balanced budget plan, which protects Medicare, Medicaid, education, and the environment." In his third and fourth responses, he also repeated the theme. It was not until Gore's fifth time to speak that he refrained from mentioning the overall theme of the Clinton/Gore ticket. In his closing statement, Gore again referred to the theme, but this time with a varied redundancy when he said: "We have a plan that will create millions more jobs, bring down the deficit further and balance the budget, while protecting Medicare, Medicaid, education, and the environment."

Jack Kemp received the first question of the debate and had 90 seconds to respond, yet he did not advance an overall theme for the campaign. Instead he chose to answer Lehrer's question by talking about having a civil discussion of issues during the debate. He also made reference to Bob Dole's World War II military experience, and he noted Lincoln's call that those who serve their party best serve the country first. As noted, Gore's rebuttal of Kemp's first answer was no rebuttal but rather an opening-speech type of response that included the Clinton/Gore campaign theme. In his 30-second response to Gore, Kemp did offer a theme long associated with the Republican party when he suggested the campaign "was about the potential of the American people to lift themselves up and not have their lives controlled by the United States Government and Washington."

Not until Kemp's fourth time to speak, however, did he reveal his major theme of the evening. The theme was offered during a rebuttal to Gore's answer about political philosophical differences between the candidates. At this point, Kemp said that he and Bob Dole wanted to "cut the tax rates across the board on each and every American, working, saving, investing and taking risks in America." Later in this answer he reiterated the call for lower taxes and added a call for lowering the capital gains tax and repealing the 83-year-old tax code. In comparison to Gore's major theme, Kemp's theme was not as apparent and vivid. Kemp could be excused for this since there was no expectation for a formal opening statement and major themes are usually introduced in opening statements. In his closing statement, however, the same lack of focus and clarity existed. For example, he called for tax reform but not tax cuts, and there is no mention of cutting or repealing the capital gains tax. His closing statement did reiterate topics mentioned earlier, but it did not succinctly reiterate a dominant, overarching theme. This was surprising, given the amount of control a candidate has over both the opening and closing statements and the fact that in closing Kemp failed to remind voters of major campaign themes, such as the 15 percent federal income tax cut. Hence, Gore was the more effective of the two candidates in stating and repeating a dominant campaign theme.

Both candidates talked about tax cuts, but Kemp placed more emphasis on this issue/theme than Gore. From a rhetorical perspective, there is reason to question the selection of a tax cut as a major debate theme. At the time of the 1996 debates, many voters had become skeptical of promises to cut taxes. *Newsweek* coverage of the Republican convention included a report that many voters were skeptical that such a promise would be honored.[15] Such skepticism was attributable, in part, to widespread public awareness that, in 1988, Republican presidential nominee George Bush promised "no new taxes" but proposed new taxes during his term as president. Four years later, Democratic nominee Bill Clinton promised a tax cut and failed to deliver a tax cut for all Americans. Those denying such skepticism pointed to Governor Christine Todd Whitman who was widely credited with winning the governorship of New Jersey because of her promise to cut taxes. However, her campaign actually dropped its tax cut message in the final weeks of her campaign and instead adopted and repeated a message that New Jersey's incumbent governor had raised taxes.[16] Thus, it was emphasis on her opponent's having raised taxes, not belief that she would cut them, that did the most for the Whitman campaign.

The second reason the call for lower taxes may have been a weak strategy is that many voters probably wondered how the federal budget deficit could be reduced while simultaneously cutting federal taxes. This call came at a time when many Americans were trying to reduce personal debt, primarily credit card debt. Realizing the difficulty of doing this, many voters wondered how debt at any level—individual, state or federal—could be reduced while income was also being reduced.[17] This issue had an immediacy and a saliency for many voters. Hence, a non-specific call by Kemp for lower taxes may have been more problematic than persuasive, especially since no specifics for cutting were discussed. This presented Kemp with a rhetorical challenge that he was unable to adequately resolve. His major theme, the tax cut, was not a new proposal and many voters wondered whether its benefits outweighed its costs.[18] Since Kemp did not address what cuts would be made, an important objection to his major theme went unanswered during the debate.

The strategy of calling for change but being non-specific is an accepted challenger strategy.[19] However, its utility in the vice presidential debate was questionable given the political climate in which new Republican majorities in Congress sought to cut government programs and federal taxes. In a sense Republicans rediscovered the political axiom that voters favor change in general but are against it in particular, especially if the particular happens to be a favorite government program such as Medicare and is linked to middle-income voters. Hence, the debates occurred in a context in which many voters were fearful of Republican calls to cut government and voters wondered whether tax cuts would mean revenue reductions in popular programs such as Medicare and Medicaid.[20] Moreover, it was because of such fear that the Clinton/Gore campaign promised to protect these federal programs for middle-income voters.

While Gore was effective in offering and repeating a dominant theme, he also attacked major themes and issues favored by the Republicans. For example, early in the debate and immediately following Kemp's contention that the American economy is "overtaxed" and "overregulated," Gore responded to a question about political philosophy with an attack message that he repeated with minor variation: "The plan from Senator Dole and Mr. Kemp is a risky, $550-billion tax scheme that actually raises taxes on 9 million of the hardest pressed working families. It would blow a hole in the deficit, cause much deeper cuts in Medicare, Medicaid, education, and the environment and knock our economy off track, raising interest rates, mortgage rates and car payments." The next opportunity Gore had to speak, he reiterated his attack by saying: "This risky scheme would blow a hole in the deficit." So not only was Gore active in stating and repeating his dominant theme, he also was quick to attack a major Kemp theme, and he did so with vivid, action-oriented language. When attacking, Gore's language was often negative as evidenced by the use of terms and phrases such as "risky tax scheme," "blow a hole in the deficit," "Blame America First," and "the biggest polluters in America."

In terms of issue goals, both candidates engaged in the strategy of linking issues to targeted audiences. For Vice President Gore, the major constituency groups were women, African Americans, urban residents, union members, teachers, retirees, and independent voters. For Kemp, it was men, whites, pro-business voters, religious conservatives, and independents. Both candidates sought to connect with these voters by linking relevant issues to specific groups and by making value-oriented appeals. Gore's appeals were also clearly directed to middle-income voters while simultaneously being intended for specific groups associated with the middle class. He appealed to specific groups by suggesting that the Clinton administration would assist them by helping them to "remain" in the middle class or to "reach" the middle class. This strategy was evident when Gore talked about providing a tax credit for college tuition, eliminating capital gains taxes on the sale of a home, offering tax breaks for first-time home buyers, and providing tax breaks for health care expenses.

The vice president also talked about middle-income issues when discussing jobs and the economy. He said: "We've had 10.5 million new jobs created in the last four years. In the last quarter the growth rate was 4.7 percent. The average growth rate is going up. It is higher than in either of the last two Republican administrations. Bob Dole said in February of this year this is the strongest economy in 30 years." In response to a question about Clinton keeping his promises, Gore again provided an answer that appealed to middle-income voters in general and targeted groups in specific. In this answer he noted that Clinton promised to create 8 million jobs and 10 million were created and that the president signed the welfare reform law and moved 1.9 million people off welfare rolls into good jobs. Gore also talked about the number of new police officers on the streets and concluded by saying that Clinton "promised middle-income tax cuts" and that "we've cut taxes for 15 million families." This answer targeted individuals, many living in urban areas, who were concerned about crime and the need for better security. It also targeted young voters seeking jobs and many middle-income workers nervous about their job security and their ability to find employment if they lost their jobs.

Kemp also targeted his answers to audiences and like Gore used economic appeals as a means to reach those targeted. He employed a challenger strategy of attacking the incumbent's record by suggesting that the economy could be better. He called the incumbent's tax plan "social engineering" and argued that the current tax code did not reflect basic Judaeo-Christian values associated with hard work, honesty, personal property, and reward for effort. In such responses, Kemp was appealing to pro-business Republicans who championed the marketplace and usually opposed government regulation of it. Comments about "social engineering" and "Judaeo-Christian" values were aimed at social and religious conservatives in the Republican party.

What emerged from the candidates' discussion of issues were two different political philosophies, ones long associated with the Republicans and Democrats. Kemp's philosophy of limited government, individual freedom, lower taxes, and capital for all Americans was evident in his appeals to middle-income voters, lower-income voters, and urban voters. As the challenger he attacked the administration for promoting policies that thwarted the application and manifestation of these principles in the lives of voters. Perhaps the best illustration of this was when he was discussing conditions in America's inner cities. He told his audience that "we really have two economies" in the country. According to Kemp, one was effective and enriching the lives of many Americans while the other, the one of the inner city, was a "socialist economy," a welfare system where there is no private housing, and parents are told where to send their children to school. As previously mentioned, he said the economy was over-taxed and overregulated and you only get a tax cut from the Clinton administration if "you do exactly what Al Gore and Bill Clinton want you to do."

For Jack Kemp, long known for his advocacy of capitalism as a primary way to deal with many of the inequities of society, the Clinton administration's policies were too restrictive and too meager to cure so many of society's ills. He illustrated this thinking in responding to the moderator's question about whether or not something was wrong with the American soul. Kemp replied that society had "the haves and the have nots." He compared the situation to the game of musical chairs in elementary school where "when the music stopped the big guy elbowed out the little guy from that last chair. That's not America folks. We need more chairs, we need a bigger table, we need a greater banquet. We need to create more wealth. We need to create more jobs and more access to credit and capital and educational choice and opportunity for any man or woman and child to be what God meant them to be, not what Washington, D.C. wants them to be." Clearly Kemp's political philosophy is revealed in these answers, a philosophy of limited but ethical government that promotes individual freedom and access to economic and educational opportunity. This philosophy was manifested in answers designed to appeal to pro-business Republicans and socially and religiously conservative Republicans. His answers also manifested his goal to appeal to a traditional Democratic constituency—low-income urban residents. This is best revealed in Kemp's answer to a question about President Clinton keeping his promises. Kemp said: "We're treading water. We have families that are hurting. We have people who are unemployed. We have people with no property. We have an administration that is demolishing public housing in our inner cities and not providing anything else but more public housing. Their solution to the inner city is more—excuse the expression but it's true, 'socialism.' "

Gore advanced a communitarian political philosophy long associated with the Democratic party.[21] Embodied in this philosophy is the belief that government should be active in creating and sustaining programs that enable American citizens to enjoy secure and productive lives. Sensitive to the possibility of being charged with being a Democrat who liked to "tax and spend," Gore amended this political philosophy to include "common-sense" approaches to problems that would result in effective programs. Like Walter Mondale in 1976, Gore advocated government actions that were people-oriented and programs that benefitted people such as tax credits for college tuition and the Family Medical Leave Act. This activist orientation toward government was evident throughout by his references to the Clinton administration's intentions: "We have a plan to...," "We have a positive plan based on three principles...," "We have a balanced budget plan...," "We have a specific plan to create...," "We have a plan to clean up two-thirds...." Like former Democrats, Gore offered an action-oriented communitarian philosophy for voters to endorse. Kemp sought many of the same goals but was guided by a political philosophy that placed individual freedom and capitalism at the foreground and limited government action in the background.

Both candidates pursued the goal of debating not to lose. Each candidate employed communication strategies associated with this goal, such as avoiding specifics, speaking in generalities, and answering a question in a way that suits a candidate.[22] Both Kemp and Gore blended these two strategies. Vice President Gore avoided answering a question about differences in political philosophy between the candidates. Rather than discussing differences about the role of government, its size, and its function in lives of people, Gore responded by saying: "The differences are very clear." This response created an expectation that he was going to talk about political philosophy and he continued by discussing the three principles of the Clinton/Gore plan: But after briefly discussing these three, Gore ignored philosophy and repeated his call for a balanced budget with "tax cuts for middle-income families," tax credits for college tuition, and tax relief for home buyers, and no capital gains taxes for selling a home. Thus, Gore's response lacked the specifics of a political philosophy but included generalities about tax cuts, tax credits, and tax relief. He did not discuss political philosophy but instead responded with a stock answer about Clinton programs.

The vice president again replied to a question the way he wanted when he was asked whether economic and foreign policies embraced by the United States had hurt the Mexican economy and caused it to devalue its peso. Gore responded with a

non-answer at first, and then later avoided the question when
he said:

No, that's not right. When Mr. Kemp started talking about the Golden
Rule, I thought he was going to talk about the gold standard again. That
used to be an integral part of this so-called "Supply Side Economics,"
but it may be something else that he now agrees with Bob Dole on,
because Bob Dole voted to take us off the gold standard, a wise vote in
my opinion. Most—all economists say if we did that, it would throw
us into a deep recession or depression and put millions out of work,
but let me come directly to this question. No, when there was a crisis
involving the Mexican peso, again President Bill Clinton showed bold
and dynamic leadership. I want to hasten to add that Senator Bob Dole
gave critical bipartisan support at the time.

Simply put, Gore avoided answering the question and did so
because he was debating not to lose. A lengthy answer about
how the Clinton administration's foreign policy contributed to
Mexico's problems was an issue with few political advantages
and one an incumbent would want to avoid, if possible, in a
political debate. This is what Gore did.

Kemp's debating not to lose was also evident when moderator
Jim Lehrer asked Kemp what he meant when he said that one
of the problems related to the lack of capital in low-income, high-
unemployment urban areas was that "all capital was in the
hands of the white people." Kemp responded by saying: "The
single greatest problem in our opinion, domestic—in the domestic economy, is that this tax code, 83 years old, a relic of the
Cold War and Hot War, inflation and depression, seven-and-a-
half million words long, overtaxes capital, overtaxes working
men and women, and families. Clearly, the Gordian knot needs
to be broken in one fell swoop." In the remainder of this answer,
one that allowed Kemp a total of 90 seconds to respond, he continued to call for a cut in taxes that would benefit American
voters such as: "Small businessmen and women, African Americans, Asian Americans, Latino Americans, [and] female Americans." At no point in his answer did he argue that capital
concentrated in white America was an obstacle to inner-city

growth and prosperity. He finally ended his answer with the reference to Niagara Falls. Kemp was known to make references to Niagara Falls when promoting capitalism for the inner cities and his use of this metaphor suggests that he employed a stock response to a question that he preferred to not answer.

IMAGE GOALS

As Friedenberg notes, "the efforts of the candidates to project their leadership qualities may well be the most important aspect of the debate."[23] This importance stems from the possibility that for a variety of reasons a vice president might become president. Kemp and certainly Gore arrived at the debate as relatively well-known public figures and did not have the burden of being unknown to voters, such as Dan Quayle or even Lloyd Bentsen had in the 1988 presidential race. Nevertheless, it was important for Gore and Kemp to be perceived as being leaders and possessing leadership qualities. Both candidates used vivid and action-oriented language to create a sense of dynamism in their actions and thoughts. Gore used action-oriented language and was careful to use the pronoun "we" as is evidenced by the following phrases that appear throughout his answers: "We've passed," "We have fought," "We are fighting," "We are determined to move forward." The use of "we" had the rhetorical advantage of linking Gore directly to the presidency. By frequently using "we" rather than "I," Gore avoided, or at least minimized, the problem of upstaging the president. Although he was careful in not upstaging President Clinton, at one point he illustrated his close proximity to the presidency and his awareness of the challenges faced by the occupant of this office when he answered a question about military action in Haiti. Gore said: "I was in the Oval Office the night President Clinton dispatched our troops from Fort Bragg. It was a tense moment."

Here Gore not only raised the specter of the presidency but also his observation and his participation with this high political office. Kemp also used action-oriented language. But it was not as pronounced as Gore's, largely because of Kemp's tendency to introduce a topic and then focus on developing support for the topic, rather than explicitly telling voters how he and Bob Dole would resolve the topic in their favor. This style of responding was evident when Kemp answered a question about whether or not government regulation had become excessive. Kemp answered by saying: "Well, we have to have the type of economic prosperity that will allow us to generate the revenues to provide this technology. Ten percent of all the emissions—10 percent of all the hydrocarbon emissions oxides going, going into the air caused by 10–100 percent of all the emissions are caused by 10 percent of the automobiles. Now there is technology that would allow infrared technology to be used to identify those cars that are providing the pollution in our atmosphere." Kemp's answer is vague and abstract. It is not about a people-oriented topic and as presented it is not audience-centered. It is a contrast to most of Gore's answers which tended to be people-oriented and audience-centered.

Another instance of Kemp's tendency to develop answers with general support without linking specific voter interests to the topic occurred when he answered a question about the relationship between economics and social order: "There is really no separation between a strong community and strong economy. And you can't have a strong economy without strong community and strong families. The word 'economics' in Greek came from the word family or law or custom of the family. A family without a job where both breadwinners are away from home and cannot spend time with their children or can't send the child to the school of their choice rather than just the choice of the federal bureaucracy." No place in the beginning of the answer does Kemp suggest action to alleviate the chronic conditions identified. While he is trying to link his answers to religious conservatives, individuals favoring limited government, and low-income and inner-city voters, it is not until the last sentence that he suggests what a President Dole might do which is to "empower public school districts and the teachers, not the federal bureaucracy at the Department of Education."

Kemp's call to empower public school districts and teachers shifted the focus from the economy to education and his answer lacked the vividness and organization of Gore's response to the same question. Gore said: "I think that economics is one of the single most important parts of the problem. That's why we're

focusing on tax credits. . . . That's why we're focusing on an economic policy. . . . We have focused especially on the most dis-
tressed areas." In this answer, Gore also discussed another
specific Clinton administration program. He said: "Another part
of it is the community development financial institution. And
the—and the law that says deposits that are made in a community, in the inner cities say, should be kept in the community,
not entirely, but some percentage of them should be kept there.
That prevents that money being taken from the community and
invested in some go-go investment on the other side of the
world." This answer offers a striking contrast to Kemp's because
Gore made a direct link between the program named and how
it helped people, whereas Kemp's answer assumed listeners
would establish such a link about the relationship between a
strong community and a strong economy.

It is well established that the image a candidate projects is
important in televised political debates. The fact that both candidates practiced in settings that simulated the televised debate
site provides evidence that both candidates were sensitive to image on television. During the actual debate Dole and Kemp
looked directly at the camera. During most answers, a reaction
shot would be taken of the candidate not answering. In the reaction shots Gore either looked at Kemp or he looked down as
he made notes. Kemp usually looked at the moderator or the
audience during reaction shots. He would also look at Gore or
make notes but not with the frequency that he looked at the
moderator. Kemp appeared to be the more energetic of the two
candidates and he achieved this through his voice and gestures.
Compared to Gore there was more variation in Kemp's voice
and he tended to place emphasis on key words and phrases, such
as "social engineering" and "Judaeo-Christian."

Kemp had more verbal fillers in his utterances than Gore. With
his energetic style, he sometimes created an image as a promoter
more than a candidate for high political office. His hand gestures
generated more movement than Gore's. His gestures were broad
and had movement outside the width of his shoulders and at
times the movement extended to his shoulders. Gore's gestures,
however, were much more constrained hand gestures and these
gestures were displayed in front of his chest. Hence, Kemp's

delivery was energetic and the source of this energy was his voice and gestures. Gore's delivery was deliberate, even prodding. He also sounded "preachy" at times, like he was lecturing a high school civics class on the virtues of some political concept. In contrast to Kemp, Gore's delivery was deliberate, his gestures were constrained and his voice lacked the variation or emphasis of Kemp's. Hence, the television images of the two candidates were different. Kemp's image was one of energy and movement, while Gore's was one of deliberateness and calm.

In terms of negative images and diminishing the image of one's opponent, the two vice presidential candidates employed different strategies. First, Kemp ignored and was criticized for not fully enacting the "attacker" role as a vice presidential challenger. Kemp's refusal to attack personal issues was significant. It was the most significant violation of an expectation for national political debates. In post-debate analysis on PBS's *Newshour*, *Wall Street Journal* reporter Paul Gigot expressed surprise that Kemp did not attack the President and his record more vigorously.[24] The reason for Kemp's reticence to attack Clinton's personal ethics stems from several factors. First, Kemp's style prior to joining the campaign had been that of an advocate for tax cuts and capitalism. Simply put, it was not his rhetorical style to attack and be negative, but rather to advocate and be positive.[25] He told Dole as much when the two met to discuss the vice presidency prior to the Republican convention. Kemp reportedly told Dole that he would not be Dole's "Agnew." Kemp's reference was to Richard Nixon's vice president, Spiro Agnew, who was willing to play the attacker role associated with a vice presidential challenger role.

Another factor for avoiding direct attacks on Clinton's personal life and legal problems stemmed from the utility of using such tactics. In 1992, George Bush attacked Clinton's ethical behavior, personal character, and trustworthiness to little avail. Moreover, Kevin Sauter points out, Dole played the role of attacker in the 1976 election and was perceived as mean, and consequently hurt his political career.[26] Another reason for not attacking Clinton's personal life was the possibility of surfacing charges that Bob Dole had an affair in the last years of his first marriage. At the time of the debate the Dole/Kemp campaign was uncertain as to whether or not the *Washington Post* was going to publish a story about the alleged affair. The Clinton/Gore campaign also possessed information about Dole's alleged affair. As a result, it is likely that Kemp was reluctant to go negative against Clinton and have Gore respond with information and charges about Dole's alleged affair.

Taken together, these factors provide a plausible explanation for why Jack Kemp did not directly attack Clinton on personal issues but instead concentrated his attacks on the programs and the policies of the Clinton administration. For example, when Gore would claim the economy was prospering, Kemp would respond by acknowledging the state of the economy but argued it would be better during a Dole/Kemp administration. The few personal attacks that Kemp did make were oblique, such as when he raised the character issue. He did so by citing Bob Dole's World War II experiences. In one answer he said that Bob Dole "crawled out of a fox hole on Riva Ridge in 1945 to save a wounded brethren." This answer invited listeners to make a comparison between Bill Clinton's efforts to avoid being drafted during the Vietnam War and Bob Dole's military experiences in World War II. In this answer Kemp was asking a lot of his audience. First, he was assuming that audience members would make such a comparison. Second, he assumed that they were familiar with the details about Clinton's efforts to avoid the military draft.

At another point Kemp raised the issue of trust, but not on a personal level. He linked trust to the tax cut issue. He noted that Clinton had promised a tax cut as a candidate in 1992 but had dropped it after he was elected, and now in another campaign Clinton had promised a tax cut again. Kemp said: "Four years too late. You told us that four years ago. And we still don't have it. How can we trust an administration that, all of the sudden, four years into or the last year of its four years tells us that now they're going to follow through on the promise they made four years ago." Thus while Kemp raised the issue of trust in this answer, he focused on the Clinton administration, not Bill Clinton the individual. Many Republicans expected Kemp as the challenger to attack Clinton's policies and personal actions. By not doing so he violated an established expectation with the role.

And unlike Gore, who repeatedly attacked and talked about such things as a "risky tax scheme," Kemp repeated his attacks infrequently.

Vice President Gore's strategy to diminish the image of the Dole/Kemp ticket was twofold. First, he sought to highlight basic inconsistencies between Dole and Kemp on issues and votes taken in the Congress. This strategy created an image of two individuals joined together on the national Republican ticket more on the basis of political expediency than on political similarity. Gore repeatedly integrated into his answers differences between Kemp and Dole. In a response to Kemp's call for radical change in the Internal Revenue Code, Gore responded that Kemp might want to check with Dole before proceeding, since Dole "wrote about 450 separate provisions in that code." At another point Gore noted that even Republican senator and Clinton nemesis Al D'Amato (R-NY) had said that Dole's proposed tax cuts "would have to cut into Medicare to pay" for the Dole/Kemp tax cut. Gore pointed out that before joining the Republican ticket, Kemp had said that "Bob Dole never met a tax that he didn't hike." Gore also noted Kemp's pre-convention endorsement of Affirmative Action and how Kemp was opposed to the California ballot initiative to repeal Affirmative Action while Dole was in favor of the initiative. Hence Gore's strategy was to drive a wedge between the two Republicans.

The second strategy used by Gore was linking Senator Dole with Speaker of the House Newt Gingrich. At the time, Gingrich was an unpopular political figure. The Clinton/Gore campaign, realizing that Kemp was popular and had helped Dole in the polls following the Republican convention, sought to make a strong connection between Dole/Gingrich rather than Dole/Kemp. Indeed the strategy for the Clinton/Gore campaign in general and the debate in particular, was to have voters associate Gingrich rather than Kemp with Dole.[27] The manifestation of this strategy is evident in three Gore debate utterances: "The environment faces dire threats from the kind of legislation that Senator Dole and Speaker Newt Gingrich tried to pass by shutting down the government and attempting to force President Clinton to accept it." Second, "We have had middle-income tax cuts on the table in the Congress and they would not—they weren't accepted by Bob Dole and Newt Gingrich because they said they would not pass them without cutting deeply into Medicare, Medicaid, education, and the environment." Third, "the Dole/ Gingrich plan on Medicare would have led to deep cuts."

POST-DEBATE STRATEGIES

When the debate was over, Kemp reportedly said to an aide, "I never want to do that again."[28] Kemp's reaction is understandable given the pressure associated with a national political debate and compounded in his case by having to debate an experienced national political debater. With the debate completed, the final phase of the entire event occurred. Both campaigns were prepared for the phase and their preparation was evidenced by their having surrogates available to talk to the media and offer explanations for their candidate's performance. A typical post-debate format for the major television networks was to have regular news anchors along with journalists and political pundits offer commentary and then to interview recognized supporters of each candidate. An example of this occurred on PBS's *Newshour* coverage of the event. In one segment of *Newshour's* coverage, Republican media consultant and former Reagan aide Michael Deaver, and Democratic media consultant Robert Shrum offered partisan interpretations. Predictably, Deaver said that Kemp "was about the best I've ever seen him," and praised the vice presidential Republican nominee's feeling, conviction, and emotion.[29] Deaver noted that Kemp had advocated a political philosophy that championed the "little guy," the "small business man," and the "low wage earner." Shrum acknowledged Kemp's earnestness but said that Gore won substantive exchanges on issues related to Medicare, environment, and education.[30] When asked whether or not the vice presidential debate changed the dynamic of the campaign, Deaver replied that Kemp was effective in enthusing Republicans and that Kemp's performance may have positively influenced Dole's poll numbers a little. Shrum replied that although Kemp had done okay, Dole was too far behind for the vice presidential debate to help Dole's candidacy in a meaningful way.

The *Newshour* special program for the vice presidential debate also had a panel that offered commentary and followed Deaver and Shrum. One panel member, Doris Kearns Goodwin, a presidential historian, bemoaned the lack of clash between the two candidates and suggested the two seemed constrained by girdles and consequently were uncomfortable with the give-and-take and thrust and parry of debates.[31] Goodwin's comment reflected her disappointment that Kemp violated the expectation that challenger candidates attack incumbents. Political writer Haynes Johnson focused his remarks on Jack Kemp and argued that Kemp had "run to the left of Clinton" in his answers and did more to appeal to some traditional Democratic voters than Gore did.[32] In particular he cited Kemp's numerous appeals to blue-collar workers, inner-city residents, and low-income voters. He noted that Kemp's appeals were a contrast to Gore's middle-income appeals. The sequencing of this program segment provided PBS with a "check" on the surrogate and likely partisan commentary of Deaver and Shrum.

The post-debate phase of the event was short-lived for several reasons. First, it was a debate between vice presidential candidates, not presidential candidates, and typically these debates do not generate as much news as presidential debates. Moreover, the next presidential debate was to be held only one week later on October 16, 1996. Thus, attention shifted to the third and final debate and how well the presidential candidates might do in a town hall format where audience members would ask questions. Visual evidence of this shift was apparent in at least one newspaper. The morning after the debate the *Louisville Courier Journal* published an article about the event and included a large side bar about the final debate.[33] Third, absent from the vice presidential debate was the sharp exchange, and/or a vivid moment that has characterized some previous vice presidential debates, such as in 1988 when Lloyd Bentsen told Dan Quayle that he was no Jack Kennedy, or 1976 when vice presidential candidate Bob Dole talked about Democratic wars. Presidential historian Doris Kearns Goodwin said the two vice presidential candidates failed to "take on" each other and that the debate was marked by a "flat civility."[34] Given President Clinton's double-digit lead in the polls prior to the debate and the uneventful and civil nature of the interaction of the vice presidential candidates, it is not surprising that the event received comparatively little post-debate media coverage.

DEBATE EFFECTS

It is well-known that the principal effect of political debates is to reinforce rather than change voter attitudes. It is also established that vice presidential debates have little if any effect on the outcome of presidential elections. However, there is some evidence to suggest that Dole's performance in 1976 hurt President Ford's chance for election and that Lloyd Bentsen's performance in 1988 may have, inadvertently, revealed Michael Dukakis as a weak candidate and consequently hurt the national Democratic ticket in 1988.[35] Overall though, voters do not base their decisions on vice presidential candidates or their debate performances.

A CNN/*USA Today*/Gallup poll of the Gore/Kemp debate revealed that Gore had won the debate by a 53 percent to 41 percent margin.[36] Another measure of the debate was a rating scale by *Campaigns and Elections* editor and publisher Ron Faucheux. Using his scorecard, Faucheux rated the debate as "just about a draw" but gave Gore the slight edge.[37] According to Faucheux, Kemp did well, but was not good enough to alter the standing in the polls between the two campaigns. The outcome between the two candidates was not surprising, and for several reasons. First, there were no memorable gaffes, or one-liners that significantly affected the outcome of the debate. Gore's response to Kemp's Niagara Falls remark was widely reported and it highlighted Gore's wit, but Kemp's remark was not a blunder and consequently had no measurable effect on the outcome. Second, and as previously mentioned, the schedule for all three debates was structured so that the media were usually commenting on one debate while previewing the next. This schedule also had the effect of reducing the amount of "spin control" after the first two debates because campaign staffs focused on preparation for the next debate. Such a shift in focus was relatively easy after the vice presidential debate since neither side produced a gaffe that required significant time for a response. Another reason for such little attention to the vice presidential debate afterward was that polling numbers remained essentially unchanged after the debate. Also, the debate was not confrontational and lacked the clash often associated with debates, and this diminished the newsworthiness of the event. Hence, soon after the vice presidential debate what became newsworthy was whether or not Dole, who was behind in the polls, would become the aggressor in the final debate.

Debate Watch Research Center conducted focus groups during and immediately after the debate.[38] Over 1,000 individuals participated in these groups and the findings suggest that many of these individuals were disappointed with the candidates' responses to the questions. In particular many participants were disappointed with the predictable and prepared answers that the candidates provided to Jim Lehrer's questions. This Debate Watch finding is not surprising given the rhetorical strategies both candidates employed in attempting to meet their issue and image goals.

Perhaps the most lasting effect of the debate for those who watched the event relates to the distinction made by the candidates regarding the party philosophy. While neither candidate provided a serious discussion and comparison of the differences in party philosophy, how the two candidates talked about functions of government during the debate revealed philosophical differences between Gore and Kemp. In a *New York Times* article published after the debate, David Rosenblum wrote: "But the fact is, if you disregard all the memorized statistics and carefully rehearsed one-liners, you can get a sense of the differences between the candidates and the parties. If they get elected, Bob Dole and Jack Kemp can be expected to do their damnedest to get Government out of peoples' hair. Bill Clinton and Al Gore, if elected, would stress the ways the government can improve peoples' lives."[39] Rosenblum's observation has merit. Like the Debate Watch focus group members, Rosenblum tired of repetitious answers. But he recognized after the debate that it was probable that voters knew basic differences between the parties and this was a lasting effect of the debate.

Another consideration regarding the debate's effects involves the impact of the event on the participants. After the 1992 vice presidential debate, Gore was perceived to possess characteristics associated with being presidential.[40] Just like in 1992, his performance in 1996 was marked by deliberate delivery and well-organized and well-supported answers. He was also aggressive in identifying and attacking inconsistencies between Dole and Kemp. In sum, he performed effectively as the incumbent vice president of the United States and in doing so established himself as the probable frontrunner for his party's presidential nomination in 2000. While Kemp's performance was not as effective as Gore's, it was without the awkwardness of Admiral Stockdale in 1992, and mistakes of President Ford in 1976. Moreover, there were moments when his performance was marked by passion and conviction. Thus, while he did not win the debate, neither did he lose in the sense of losing an academic debate. The event made him visible to millions of Americans and because of his performance, he positioned himself to be a leading contender for the Republican presidential nomination in 2000, should he choose to run.

A final effect of the debate is one that has been suggested by Harvard historian Michael Bechloss. According to Bechloss, because of the debates, the caliber of vice presidential candidates has improved.[41] His contention has merit. In the past, serious consideration was given to geographical balance in selecting vice presidents. This occurred in 1960 when Richard Nixon of California selected Henry Cabot Lodge of Massachusetts as a running mate. Another example occurred in 1988 when Michael Dukakis of Massachusetts selected Lloyd Bentsen of Texas as a running mate. In recent years, especially after Quayle's debate with Bentsen in 1988 and Stockdale's debate performance in 1992, the ability to be effective in a vice presidential debate has become an important consideration in selecting a running mate. This is a positive change for national elections because participating in a national debate before millions of viewers is a pressure situation and requires candidates to think and act in a challenging context. While "canned" answers can detract from a debate, many answers are not "canned" or stock answers. In the future, debate formats can be amended to minimize this problem so that audiences may observe candidates as they advance, defend, and attack important questions in a debate before an election is held. Surely this type of activity has more identification with the role of vice president than one's geographical location. Hence, Bechloss's contention does have merit and is a likely positive debate effect.

CONCLUSION

In the conclusion to his study of the 1976 Mondale-Dole vice presidential debate, Kevin Sauter writes that "it seems safe to conclude that it would have been nearly impossible for Dole to have won."[42] It is ironic that the same conclusion may be made for the 1996 vice presidential debate between Gore and Kemp. There is a paradox in that Dole was criticized in 1976 for being too aggressive and mean in the vice presidential debate while 20 years later his own running mate, Jack Kemp, would be criticized for being too passive and civil in the same context.

Kemp had little chance to "win" the debate and influence the outcome of the election. There are three main reasons that Kemp had little chance for success. First, his opponent was well prepared, and experienced in national political debate, and not prone to making mistakes. Simply put, it was unlikely that Kemp, as a novice in national political debate, was going to perform better than Al Gore. He did not. Second, Kemp did not have significant issues on his side. He was debating at a time when the economy was robust and the country was not facing any foreign policy crises. Many people expected him to attack President Clinton on personal issues, but with the threat of Dole's alleged affair being made public and with the knowledge that the Clinton campaign was aware of this information, Kemp could not have effectively attacked Clinton on such issues. Had he done so, Gore could have rebutted Kemp with attacks on Dole's personal life. The information on Dole would have been more newsworthy than information on Clinton, since the information on Dole was new. Hence, Kemp did not have major, salient issues to discuss that would help win. Third, even had he "won" the debate, with the Clinton/Gore ticket enjoying a double-digit lead in the polls, it was unlikely that Kemp's debating effort could influence the polls significantly and positively for the Dole/Kemp campaign for more than a few days. Thus, Kemp, the positive and eager challenger, did about as well as possible considering all the variables that were not in his favor. It is certain that his message could have been more focused and his role as the "attacker" more thorough, but even if these factors had been present it is unlikely that they would have changed the outcome of the debate.

NOTES

1. "Transcript of the 1996 Vice Presidential Debate," Commission on Presidential Debates, Washington, D.C., October 9, 1996 (www. debates96.org). All subsequent citations quoting directly from the debate were taken from this transcript.

2. *Inside Debates: A Resource Guide* (Washington, D.C.: Commission on Presidential Debates, 1996).

3. Howard Fineman, "Does Dole Have a Prayer," *Time*, October 14, 1996, p. 30.

4. Charles Babington and Paul Duggan, "Gore, Kemp Debate Could Preview Race for White House," *Washington Post*, October 9, 1996, p. A-16.

5. "Kid Gloves," *Newsweek*, November 18, 1996, p. 117.

6. Ibid.

7. Babington and Duggan, "Gore, Kemp Debate Could Preview Race for White House," p. A-16.

8. Ibid.

9. John Meyer and Diana B. Carlin, "The Impact of Formats on Voter Reaction," in *The 1992 Presidential Debates in Focus*, ed. Diana B. Carlin and Mitchell S. McKinney (Westport, Conn.: Praeger, 1993), p. 81.

10. Frances R. Matera and Michael B. Salwen, "Unwieldy Questions? Circuitous Answers? Journalists as Panelists in Presidential Election Debates," *Journal of Broadcasting and Electronic Media* 40 (Summer 1996): 309–317.

11. Diana B. Carlin and Peter J. Bicak, "Toward a Theory of Vice Presidential Debate Purposes," *Argumentation and Advocacy* 30 (Fall 1993): 119–130.

12. Albert R. Hunt, "Jack Kemp, the Happy Warrior," *Wall Street Journal*, August 15, 1996, p. A-15.

13. David E. Rosenbaum, "A Passion for Ideas: Jack French Kemp," *New York Times Biographical Service*, August 1996, pp. 1188–1190.

14. "Masters of the Message," *Time*, November 18, 1996, p. 83.

15. Joe Klein, "Playing the Squeeze," *Newsweek*, August 26, 1996, p. 29.

16. Ibid.

17. "Consumers Resist Holiday Urge to Say Charge It," *The Cincinnati Enquirer*, January 10, 1997, p. B-12.

18. Dick Morris, *Behind the Oval Office: Winning the Presidency in the Nineties* (New York: Random House, 1997), p. 313.

19. Judith S. Trent and Robert V. Friedenberg, *Political Campaign Communication: Principles and Practices*, 3rd ed. (Westport, Conn.: Praeger, 1995), p. 82.

20. "Newt's Second Chance," *Newsweek*, November 18, 1996, p.16.

21. Kurt W. Ritter, "American Political Rhetoric and the Jeremiad Tradition: Presidential Nomination Acceptance Addresses, 1960–1976," *Central States Speech Journal* 31 (1980): 153–171.

22. Robert V. Friedenberg, "Patterns and Trends in National Political Debates," in *Rhetorical Studies of National Political Debates: 1960–1992*, ed. Robert V. Friedenberg (Westport, Conn.: Praeger, 1994), p. 241.

23. Friedenberg, "Patterns and Trends in National Political Debates," p. 253.

24. Paul Gigot, PBS, "*Newshour*'s Special Election Coverage of the 1996 Presidential Campaign," October 9, 1996.

25. Hunt, "Jack Kemp, the Happy Warrior."

26. Kevin Sauter, "The 1976 Mondale-Dole Vice Presidential Debate," in *Rhetorical Studies of National Political Debates: 1960–1992*, ed. Robert V. Friedenberg (Westport, Conn.: Praeger, 1994), p. 65.

27. Morris, *Behind the Oval Office*, p. 332.

28. "Kid Gloves," p. 117.

29. Michael Deaver, PBS, "*Newshour*'s Special Election Coverage of the 1996 Presidential Campaign," October 9, 1996.

30. Robert Shrum, PBS, "*Newshour*'s Special Election Coverage of the 1996 Presidential Campaign," October 9, 1996.

31. Doris Kearns Goodwin, PBS, "*Newshour*'s Special Election Coverage of the 1996 Presidential Campaign," October 9, 1996.

32. Haynes Johnson, PBS, "*Newshour*'s Special Election Coverage of the 1996 Presidential Campaign," October 9, 1996.

33. "Gore, Kemp Differ Sharply," *Louisville Courier Journal*, October 10, 1996, pp. A-1, A-6.

34. Goodwin, PBS, "*Newshour*'s Special Election Coverage," October 9, 1996.

35. Carlin and Bicak, "Toward a Theory of Vice Presidential Debate Purposes," p. 119.

36. Justin C. Oppmann, "Poll Says Gore Clear Winner in Debates," Internet, All Politics (www.all politics.com), October 10, 1996.

37. Ron Faucheux, "The Vice Presidential Debate: A Scorecard," *Congressional Quarterly Covers The 1996 Debates* (www.americanvoter.com), October 10, 1996.

38. "V.P. Debate Watch Results," press release, Debate Watch Research Center, University of Kansas, October 13, 1996.

39. David E. Rosenbaum, "In a Debate, It's Themes, Not Facts," *New York Times*, October 13, 1996, Sec. 4, p. 6.

40. Carlin and Bicak, "Toward a Theory of Vice Presidential Debate Purposes," p. 128.

41. Michael Bechloss, PBS, "*Newshour*'s Special Election Coverage of the 1996 Presidential Campaign," October 9, 1996.

42. Sauter, "The 1976 Mondale-Dole Vice Presidential Debate," p. 65.

SELECT BIBLIOGRAPHY

Note: This chapter was written six weeks after the election, consequently little substantive material about the vice presidential debate was available at the time.

Carlin, Diana B., and Peter J. Bicak. "Toward a Theory of Vice Presidential Debate Purposes." *Argumentation and Advocacy* 30 (Fall 1993): 119–130. This article provides an illuminating focus on vice presidential debates and considers the different challenges, purposes, and potentialities of this debate compared to presidential debates.

"Kid Gloves." *Newsweek*, November 18, 1996, pp. 112–117. This article about the presidential debates appeared in *Newsweek*'s "Special Election Issue" and provides information about how Gore and Kemp prepared for their debate.

Martel, Myles. *Political Campaign Debates: Images, Strategies, and Tactics.* New York: Longman, 1983. Although dated, Martel's discussion of strategies and tactics used by candidates for participating in political debates continues to be an excellent source.

"Masters of the Message." *Time*, November 18, 1996, pp. 77–96. This article in *Time*'s "Election Special" issue provides insight about how polls were used to shape dominant themes and messages in the Clinton/Gore campaign, including the debates. This article also discusses the difficulty the Dole/Kemp campaign had in selecting major themes.

Debate Transcripts

"Transcript of the 1996 Vice Presidential Debate." Commission on Presidential Debates, Washington D.C., October 9, 1996 (www.debates96.org).

Chapter 3

Patterns and Trends in National Political Debates: 1960–1996

Robert V. Friedenberg

The preceding chapters by Professors Kathleen Kendall and Gaut Ragsdale focused on the 1996 national political debates. Hence, this volume serves as a worthy updating and extension of its similarly titled companion volume, which contains comparable studies of each of the ten national political debates held between 1960 and 1992.[1] These chapters and their predecessor studies in the companion volume have addressed such questions as:

1. What factors motivated the candidates to debate?
2. What were the goals of each candidate in debating?
3. What were the rhetorical strategies utilized by each candidate?
4. What were the effects of the debates?

Aware of the overwhelming importance of television as a political medium, Kendall's work examines the 1996 presidential debates by focusing on how the media presented topics such as the candidates' goals, the candidates' strategies, and the effects of the debate on the public. The rhetoric she examines is not only that of the candidates, but also that of the media commentators.

Ragsdale examines similar topics, but his focus is clearly on the rhetoric of the candidates. This chapter will draw on their studies as well as the earlier studies found in the companion volume to this one, to examine the patterns and trends that have evolved in national political debates since 1960.

CANDIDATE MOTIVATION TO DEBATE

In 1960, the circumstances discussed by Theodore Windt caused both Senator John F. Kennedy and Vice President Richard Nixon to engage in political debates.[2] That combination of circumstances did not materialize again until 1976. Although debates were not held in 1964, 1968, and 1972, speculation about them took place, caused no doubt by both the memories of the 1960 presidential debates and the proliferation of political debates in campaigns for lesser offices.

In 1976, President Ford and Governor Carter agreed not only to a series of debates, but to allow their vice presidential candidates to also debate. In retrospect, the 1976 election seems pivotal in institutionalizing political debates for three reasons.

First, 1976 marks the first time that an incumbent president engaged in political debates. Although Ford was an unelected president who was not in the normal defensive posture of an incumbent, defending his own record, he was nevertheless an incumbent. At the conclusion of the 1976 campaign, much of the conventional wisdom concerning an incumbent president debating no longer seemed quite so valid. In the course of his series of debates with Governor Carter, Ford had neither given away state secrets nor been at a handicap by virtue of his knowledge of such secrets. The oft-voiced concerns, that an incumbent debating foreign policy might put the nation at risk, seemed far less valid after 1976.

Ford issued his challenge to debate Carter when he trailed the Georgia governor by approximately 30 points in most public opinion polls.[3] It was the challenger candidate, Carter, whose credibility to serve as president was enhanced as a consequence of these debates. It is this very problem, that by the very act of debating a challenger the incumbent enhances the credibility of the challenger, that traditionally contributed to the reluctance of incumbents to debate. Nevertheless, Ford closed Carter's 30-point lead during the period of time when the debates were being held, eventually losing by only 2 percent of the vote. While the increased credibility that Carter may have gained from the debates no doubt worked to his advantage, clearly it could not have been decisive in the election. For, at the very time that Carter may have been gaining credibility from the debates, Ford was closing the gap between the two men. Hence, the oft-voiced concern that incumbents will suffer because the very act of debating their challengers vests those challengers with credibility was diminished by the 1976 campaign. Although Carter's credibility was enhanced by the debates, the importance of that increased credibility seems to have been minimal.

Thus, the first reason that 1976 was a pivotal year in the institutionalization of political debates is that it forced a rethinking about the nature of incumbency and political debates. Two of the principal reasons incumbents avoided political debates did not seem as valid in the wake of the 1976 experience as they had previously. In 1976, an incumbent president debated without any appreciable harm being done to American foreign policy. In 1976, an incumbent president debated and thereby perhaps contributed to his opponent's growth in credibility during the campaign. Nevertheless, Carter's increased credibility did not seem to translate into an increase in his popularity vis-à-vis Ford.

The second reason that 1976 was a pivotal year in the institutionalization of political debates was that a candidate who had debated would seek reelection four years later. In 1960, Kennedy had debated, but his assassination meant that in 1964 Lyndon Johnson was the incumbent. In 1980, Jimmy Carter sought reelection. As Kurt Ritter and David Henry have illustrated, having chosen to debate in 1976 made it extremely awkward for Carter to avoid debating in 1980.[4]

As we have seen, several of the reasons typically offered by incumbents to avoid debating lost their importance after Ford's participation in the 1976 debates. Moreover, Carter had himself favored debates when he perceived them to be advantageous in 1976. Consequently, he might well have expected a highly negative public reaction had he avoided debating in 1980. This was especially true in light of his failure to debate during the Democratic primaries, in contrast to challenger Ronald Reagan's willingness to debate both in the Republican primaries and early in the general election against third-party candidate John Anderson. Had Carter failed to debate Ronald Reagan, the public might well have perceived Carter as a weak president unable to defend the poor policies of his administration.

His participation in the 1976 debates contributed to placing Carter under considerable pressure to debate in the 1980 general election. When Carter acquiesced to that pressure, the nation for the first time experienced political debates in two successive presidential elections. Public expectations were being conditioned to expect presidential debates. That conditioning began in earnest in 1976, and by 1980 had seemingly made it impossible for a man to debate in one election and avoid debating in the next without suffering badly in the public's mind.

The final reason that 1976 was a pivotal year in the institutionalization of political debates is that it marked the introduction of vice presidential debates. In their enthusiasm to aggressively challenge Jimmy Carter, who was well ahead of President Ford, the Ford/Dole campaign arranged, shortly after Ford had challenged Carter to debate, for Senator Robert Dole to challenge his counterpart, Senator Walter Mondale, to a debate. As Kevin Sauter has ably illustrated, that decision seems to have been made without fully considering the position in which it placed Senator Dole.[5]

The precedent for vice presidential debates set in 1976 has been followed in five of our last six national elections, including the last four in a row. The only exception was in 1980, when Carter's reluctance to debate delayed the presidential debates until very late in the campaign. Thus, because 1976 witnessed an incumbent president breaking with tradition to debate, because 1976 witnessed a candidate who debated and who would run again four years later, and because 1976 witnessed the first vice presidential debate, it is a pivotal year in the institutionalization of national political debates.

In 1980, a reluctant Jimmy Carter debated Ronald Reagan. Carter's strategists, particularly Patrick Caddell, felt that debating was not in his best interests. On October 14, as Ritter and Henry note, they considered attempting to sabotage debate negotiations by delivering an ultimatum to Reagan that they felt would force him to reject debating. Yet, ultimately Carter debated Reagan. No doubt public opinion played a major role in the Carter campaign deliberations. October polls showed the public increasingly desirous of a debate and by significant majorities expressing their disapproval of Carter's reluctance to debate. By 1980, the public's expectations that presidential candidates would debate emerged as a significant factor candidates had to consider when determining whether or not to debate.

As Craig Smith and Kathy Smith ably illustrate, in 1984 an incumbent president, with an overwhelming lead in both the public opinion polls and the electoral college, chose to debate.[6] As early as 1960, Richard Nixon's decision to debate had been based in part on his concern for the negative public reaction that he perceived would result from refusing to debate. That Ronald Reagan debated Walter Mondale in 1984 suggests a shift in the nature of public expectations regarding presidential candidates in the years since 1960. It is entirely fair to suggest, as Smith and Smith do, that by 1984, even an incumbent president with a commanding lead could not withstand public pressure to debate. Although, as Smith and Smith also acknowledge, Reagan's actor-ego and other factors may have also contributed to his decision to debate, nevertheless, the role of public opinion cannot be minimized.

Thus, by 1988 the editors of *Time* magazine observed that political debates had become an inevitable feature of our presidential campaigns.[7] Since 1988, *Time*'s observation has been validated. In 1996, though the two principal candidates argued over the details of timing and format, and though the Commission on Presidential Debates had to determine the appropriateness of including third-party candidates, there was never any doubt that President Clinton and Senator Dole, as well as their running mates, would debate. By 1996 it was a given that major party candidates would debate. Primarily because of public expectations, presidential debates, and to a large extent vice presidential debates, have become an institutionalized feature of America's national political campaigns.

CANDIDATE GOALS IN DEBATING

Since no two elections are identical, the goals which candidates have in political debates necessarily differ. However, since 1960 some goals have consistently surfaced as candidates and their strategists think about political debates. Those goals can be understood when we realize that they are of two distinct types. Candidates develop issue goals for debates. Candidates develop image goals for debates.

Issue Goals

Issues vary from debate to debate. Today Americans under the age of 40 could scarcely identify the islands of Quemoy and Matsu, much less attach significance to them. Yet, in 1960, they were of vital concern not only to Kennedy and Nixon, but to the entire nation. Similarly, it is likely that within a few years, the few Americans who recognize the name Willie Horton will more likely identify him as the power-hitting Detroit Tiger outfielder of the 1960s than as the convicted murderer of the same name who left jail under the Massachusetts prisoner furlough program, committed heinous crimes in Maryland, and became notorious throughout the nation in 1988, when that furlough program was used by George Bush as an example of Michael Dukakis's soft stand on crime. Nevertheless, though issues vary from debate to debate, most candidates develop similar issue-oriented goals for their debates.

As Myles Martel has observed, "in high level, heavily-financed campaigns involving potentially decisive debates, specific goals designated for targeted audience segments are, naturally, more likely to be well formulated than in lower level campaigns."[8] That is, candidates will target audience segments that are vital for their success, and treat specific issues that are designed to appeal to these targeted audiences. For example, as Windt illustrates, at the time of the first debate, Kennedy realized that he needed far greater support from the black community if he was to win. Moreover, as Windt illustrated, Kennedy had targeted other constituent groups to whom he wished to appeal during the debate. Similarly, as Ritter and Henry observed, in 1980, Carter and his strategist developed a list of three major voting blocs and two secondary voting blocs to whom the president was to aim his remarks.

As Kathleen Kendall and Gaut Ragsdale have indicated in their studies of the 1996 debates, both Democratic Party candidates, Clinton and Gore, targeted women voters with their remarks. That both were effective with this unusually large target group may have contributed appreciably to their success in these debates. Targeting audiences and treating issues in the debate so as to have maximum impact among targeted audiences is the first issue goal consistently used in national political debates.

The second issue goal commonly used in national political debates is to develop a broad, inclusive, overall theme with which most voters can identify. As Halford Ryan illustrated, in his study of the 1988 presidential debates, George Bush's principal goal that year was to juxtapose his values with Dukakis's values, thereby developing his overall theme that he was far more conservative than the liberal Massachusetts governor, and hence much more attuned to the goals and aspirations of most Americans.[9] Dan Hahn and Pat Devlin have well illustrated the success that Bill Clinton and Al Gore had in developing an overall theme in their 1992 debates. Their studies of those debates reflect Clinton and Gore consistently attempting to suggest that it was time for a change, particularly with respect to government economic policies.[10] The overarching theme utilized by these two Democratic candidates in 1992 was virtually the same utilized in the first presidential debates by John Kennedy who argued, in 1960, that though the country was doing well, it was not doing well enough.

In 1996, having governed for four years, Clinton and Gore developed a new overall theme when they debated. As Kendall and Ragsdale indicate, both Democratic candidates stressed a "focused tax cut," while striving to preserve fundamental government services. As Ragsdale points out, Gore was especially effective in consistently reiterating the overall Democratic theme that "We have a plan to balance the budget while protecting Medicare, Medicaid, education and the environment." The importance of a debater consistently reiterating an overarching message is emphasized by Kendall's conclusion that "there was little attention" given by the networks "to the nature and quality of the arguments and evidence used in the debates." With network coverage stressing the horse race nature of the debates, and network commentators, as Kendall illustrated, making generalized assessments, it becomes increasingly important for the candidates to repeatedly stress their major idea. Thus, the development of an overall theme which is sufficiently broad and inclusive enough to appeal to most of the voters is a second common goal of national political debaters. As Ragsdale suggests, in 1996 it may well have been Al Gore, more than any of the other three candidates, who remained intently focused on his overarching message.

A third issue-related goal of most political debaters is playing not to lose. At first glance, this goal seems appropriate only to the candidate who enjoys a comfortable lead. Such a candidate could, understandably, seek to avoid the major controversies that fresh new specific policy proposals might entail.

But why would candidates running behind in the campaign also choose this goal? They, too, often debate not to lose. The answer is a function of the nature of national political debates. These debates have become potentially the most significant 90 minutes in campaigns which have come to occupy literally years of effort by candidates, their families, and staffs. Speaking to the largest audiences they will ever address, in a situation that creates far more drama than virtually any other speaking situation they will ever face, few candidates, even those that are behind, are inclined to take risks. Risks, even for candidates who trail in the election, are simply too great to take in the high stakes arena of national political debates.

This fear of failure seems to have intensified in the wake of press coverage of President Ford's so-called Eastern European gaffe. As Goodwin Berquist's study illustrates, most Americans might have totally ignored Ford's remark without the intensive press attention it received. Yet, as Kendall's study of our most recent presidential debates illustrates, such coverage is a routine aspect of contemporary national political debating. Although the networks rarely examine arguments in detail, Kendall found that the debates themselves, not the debates as part of an ongoing campaign, were often treated extensively as lead stories. Moreover, prior experience indicates that if a candidate makes a clear error, the networks will stress that moment of the debate, often to the exclusion of any serious analysis of the remainder of the debate. The intense scrutiny of a debate error contributes heavily to the desire of candidates to play safe, to play not to lose.

As Ragsdale illustrated, this was particularly true in the 1996 vice presidential debate where he found both Gore and Kemp engaging in the principal means employed by candidates to avoid losing. Ragsdale reports that both vice presidential candidates avoided specifics and spoke in generalities. Moreover, he found that both often avoided directly answering the questions posited by moderator Jim Lehrer, preferring to interpret the questions in such a manner that they could utilize a prepared response to appeal to a targeted audience.

Image Goals

The second group of candidate goals in national political debates is related to the images that candidates seek to project to the voters. National political debates offer candidates an excellent opportunity to affect those images. Debates attract viewers who may have never before observed the candidate seriously. Such viewers have images of the candidates that are often not well formed, and are amenable to change. Hence, it is only natural that candidates develop image goals for national political debates. Typically, the image goals of candidates include: (1) creating a more positive image of themselves, (2) creating a more negative image of their opponent, (3) positively modifying existing images of themselves, and (4) negatively modifying existing images of their opponents.

One or more of these four image goals has been among the goals of virtually every contemporary national political debater. Because they are normally less well-known, and hence have less of a public image, vice presidential candidates tend to place great emphasis on image goals. In his insightful study of the first vice presidential debates, Kevin Sauter observes that in 1976, both Walter Mondale and Robert Dole shared a goal central to their vice presidential debate: impressing the voters with their presidential potential. Because they are often comparatively unknown, vice presidential candidates may have vague or ambiguous images with the public. Hence, they tend to focus their image goals on building a positive image of themselves. This was certainly a major goal of both Mondale and Dole, and as studies have illustrated, of virtually every vice presidential debater.[11]

By the time they engage in presidential debates, most presidential candidates are reasonably well-known, and already have firmly established images with the public. Consequently, presidential image goals often involve modifying existing images. In 1960, John Kennedy sought to modify his image as an inexperienced leader. In 1980, Ronald Reagan sought to modify his image as an overly aggressive, war-prone hawk.

In 1996, Senator Robert Dole's image for many Americans was that of an aggressive political attack dog who, as when he debated Walter Mondale 20 years earlier, might well take the low road in the debates. As Kendall illustrates, prior to the debates, press reports might have contributed to the impression of an aggressive Dole, focusing on possible Dole campaign tactics such as inviting fired White House Travel Director Billy Dale to the debate, or raising questions about Clinton's alleged ethical lapses.

As a challenger candidate, clearly Dole had to attack the President. But Dole limited his attacks to what the public generally perceived as legitimate questions of the President's policies. Moreover, he made frequent and effective use of humor. This approach may well have contributed to modifying his image.

Political observers have been virtually unanimous in noting the growth of negative campaigning in our last few elections. Hence, it should not surprise us to find that recent debates have witnessed many attempts at creating negative opponent images and negatively modifying opponent images.

Recognizing that few people vote for vice presidents, most vice presidential candidates have focused their negative image goals not on their opponents, but rather on the opposing presidential candidate. As Judith Trent illustrated in her study of the 1984 vice presidential debate, Congresswoman Geraldine Ferraro attempted to portray Reagan as cold and unsympathetic to the poor, rather than the warm-hearted, even-handed leader America needed.[12] As Devlin illustrates, the principal goal of Dan Quayle in the 1992 vice presidential debate was to portray Clinton as a man who was unworthy of America's trust.

In 1996, both Jack Kemp and Al Gore attempted to discredit the image of the opposing presidential candidate. As Ragsdale points out, Kemp had difficulty in discrediting Clinton's image for a variety of reasons. Ragsdale found that it simply was not Kemp's style to attack, that Kemp was likely aware that similar tactics had not worked for Republicans in 1992, and that to attack Clinton personally might cause Democrats to surface allegations about an alleged Dole affair. Ragsdale found that Gore was more effective in discrediting Dole. Gore offered examples of sharp differences between Kemp and Dole, creating the image of a Republican ticket concocted out of political expediency rather than similar political philosophy. Moreover, Gore continually linked Dole to the unpopular Republican Speaker of the House, Newt Gingrich.

Even when vice presidential candidates have focused on the image of their counterparts, they have done so as a means of questioning the wisdom of the opposing presidential candidate. As Trent has observed, in 1984 Vice President George Bush, debating the only woman to ever engage in a national political debate, Geraldine Ferraro, acted condescending or patronizing. To the extent that his portrayal of her as poorly qualified and inexperienced not only served to tarnish her image, it would also negatively modify the image of the man who selected her, Walter Mondale. Moreover, Mondale had trouble shaking the image of being little more than a tool of labor, feminists, and other special interests within the Democratic Party. That negative image of Mondale was reinforced if Bush's patronizing behavior conveyed to viewers that Ferraro was inexperienced and ill qualified.

In like manner, as Decker has observed in his study of the 1988 vice presidential debate, one of Democratic vice presidential candidate Lloyd Bentsen's principal goals was to portray Republican Dan Quayle as too shallow to serve as president.[13] To the extent that he succeeded, he not only helped create a negative image of the Indiana senator, but he undermined the wisdom of this crucial Bush decision, thus negatively modifing Bush's image as an experienced, reliable leader.

In 1996, neither vice presidential candidate attempted to question the ability of his opponent and thereby undermine the opposing presidential candidate who had selected him. Kemp could scarcely do so, given that his opponent had already served for four years. Moreover, Gore could scarcely raise questions about Kemp's fundamental competency, given that Kemp had served as both a congressman and cabinet member, and was himself widely perceived to be a credible presidential candidate, an office he had once briefly sought and which many had widely suggested he seek in 1996.

Robert Weiss has argued that in political debates, images and issues "intertwine in all manner of convolutions and mutually affect one another in countless ways."[14] Weiss's observation is undeniable, as candidates frequently respond to issues in ways designed to advance one or more of the four image-related goals that characterize contemporary political debates.

RHETORICAL STRATEGIES IN NATIONAL POLITICAL DEBATES

The results of political debates are ultimately a function of what the public perceives. Consequently, national campaigns typically attempt to condition public perceptions of an upcoming debate prior to the event itself. Moreover, they attempt to shape the interpretation of the debate, once the event is over. Consequently, any discussion of rhetorical strategies must consider not only those strategies utilized by the debaters during the debate, but also those that are utilized on their behalf both before and after the debate.

Pre-Debate Strategies

Candidates in national political debates have typically engaged in three pre-debate strategies. The first two involve the candidate. The third is primarily a function of the candidate's staff.

First, the candidate prepares. Just as different individuals prepare differently for speaking situations, so, too, do candidates prepare differently for debate situations. Nevertheless, it would appear that the most effective political debaters invariably include as part of the preparation process an oral rehearsal of the questions they anticipate. As Windt observed in his study of the 1960 debates, and on the basis of his own experience coaching political debaters, mental rehearsal by candidates is rarely as useful as oral rehearsal. It is probably more than coincidence that candidates who have done well in debates, such as Kennedy in 1960, Reagan in 1980 and in his second 1984 debate, Ferraro in 1984, Bush in 1988, and Clinton in 1992, spent considerable time in oral rehearsals and mock debates. Moreover, it is probably more than coincidence that many of the debaters who had considerable difficulty in their encounters, Nixon in the first 1960 debate, Dole in the 1976 vice presidential debate, and Dukakis in 1988, were all either unable or reluctant to engage in extensive oral rehearsals and mock debates.

The importance of practice was a lesson well learned by the participants in the 1996 debates. As Kendall and Ragsdale both illustrated, all four participants took time from their campaign schedules to prepare. Moreover, all four prepared by engaging in mock debates which required answering questions orally and then evaluating and refining their answers.

Second, candidates recognize that they are debating on television and not simply in an auditorium. Those who prepare accordingly typically fare better. Such preparation consists of considering the many variables involved in a television appearance, and calmly making reasoned decisions about how to best handle each variable. Those variables include such things as: (1) the type of dress, (2) the type of make-up, (3) when to maintain eye contact with the opponent, the panel, or the camera, (4) whether to sit or stand at the lectern, and (5) what Martel calls "stage tactics" to use when walking on stage, greeting the opponent, or waiting for the debate to open.[15] Ronald Reagan, who was enormously successful in televised debates, is often perceived to have had the advantage of a first career before the cameras prior to his political career. While that experience no doubt was an advantage, what is often overlooked or overshadowed by Reagan's prior career is the meticulous concern for the variables of television that characterized his preparation for televised debates.[16]

Again, these lessons were well learned by the four 1996 debaters. Although all adapted well to television, they did project differently. Ragsdale notes that this was especially true of the two vice presidential candidates. He concludes that Kemp projected energy and movement, while Gore projected deliberateness and calm.

The final pre-debate strategy engaged in by many candidates and their staffs is attempting to lower public expectations of their performance. If prior expectations are low, it may not require a strong effort by the candidate to appear to have done well in the debate. Moreover, if the candidate is expected to do poorly, and does in fact do well, it may resound as a major victory whose very unexpectedness gives the entire campaign a big lift. Consequently, because the candidate who is perceived to have won the debate is in part a function of what people expect, many candidates seek to lower public expectations of their debate performance.[17]

The impact of John Kennedy's 1960 first debate "victory" was magnified by the expectation that he would have difficulty in holding his own with Richard Nixon, whose reputation was based in no small part on his television and debating skills, evidenced in his 1952 "Checkers" address and his 1959 "kitchen debates" with Soviet Premier Nikita Khrushchev. Significantly, Kennedy's campaign did not publicly boast of their candidate's highly successful debate in his first successful bid for the Senate. Although key Kennedy strategists were highly sensitive to the many analogies between 1952 and 1960, they did not make a point of publicizing the fact that in 1952 Kennedy had more than held his own while debating another far more experienced Republican, Henry Cabot Lodge, who was well-known for his mastery of foreign affairs and who, in 1960, ironically found himself again running against Kennedy, this time as Richard Nixon's vice presidential nominee.[18] In 1960, Kennedy won the expectations game, and perhaps, with it, the debates and the election.

Kendall illustrates well that Clinton and Dole both played the expectations game in 1996. She found that, prior to the first debate, Clinton told reporters that his preparation was being limited by his need to prepare for the Mideast summit. Moreover, she found his aids sharing with the media, and through them the public, Clinton's inability to keep his answers short as the rules required, thus lowering expectations. Similarly, she notes that the media filed reports prior to the first debate in which Dole was lavish with his praise of Clinton's debating ability. Both men had learned the lessons of past debaters.

Strategies for the Debate

The strategies used by candidates during the debate itself are largely a function of the specific goals each candidate has set. Consequently, this section will examine debate strategies by suggesting the common strategies utilized by candidates to implement the principal debate goals discussed earlier. Because goals can be well understood by thinking of them as issue goals and image goals, strategies will be treated in a like manner.

Issue-Oriented Debate Strategies

The first common goal of national political debaters is to target specific audiences and then to treat issues that will have maximum impact on the targeted audiences. Typically, this is accomplished through the utilization of several strategies. First, it can be accomplished through the opening and closing statements. The only time during the entire debate over which the candidates have complete control are those few moments when they are given the opportunity to make opening and closing remarks. Consequently, often these remarks are planned to appeal directly to targeted audiences. In 1992, in each of his concluding statements, Clinton targeted both the economically disadvantaged and those concerned for their economic futures, telling the American public that it was time for changes in our economic policies. In 1996, he targeted women in the opening statement of his first debate by making eighteen references to legislation and issues that were more salient to women than to men, and only six references to issues that were more salient to men than to women.[19]

A second common strategy utilized to facilitate appeals to target audiences is well illustrated in Decker's analysis of the Quayle-Bentsen debates. Decker found what he characterized as a poor fit between the questions and the answers. In effect, as his study illustrates, Quayle and Bentsen, like many candidates before them, were forcing the questions to fit their answers, rather than fitting their answers to the questions. In this manner, they could treat the issues they wished to treat.

When Quayle was asked about subsidy payments to farmers, he responded by discussing Carter's grain embargo and Dukakis's admiration for Belgian endive as the crop of the future. When Bentsen was asked about the Occupational Safety and Health Administration, he responded by discussing James Watt and the environmental protection practices of the Reagan-Bush administration. Quayle and Bentsen stand in a long line of candidates who realize that a moderator or panelists may not ask questions that enable them to address the audiences they have targeted. One approach is to answer the question. The other, widely practiced, is to make the question fit the prepared answer, thus addressing the concerns of a targeted constituency. A question about subsidy payments to large farmers and agrobusinessmen, a relatively small constituency, thus elicits an answer that relates to small farmers and small-farm-related businessmen, a large targeted constituency for Quayle. A question which addresses concerns of the business community, a largely Republican constituency, thus elicits an answer that relates to environmentalists, a targeted Democratic constituency whose concerns Bentsen wishes to address in the debate.

In like manner, in 1980, President Carter's strategists even developed a standard pattern for answering debate questions which facilitated fitting the questions to the answers. As Ritter and Henry illustrate, Carter first determined which targeted audience he wished to address with the answer and often began his answer with a preamble announcing his targeted audience. This preamble was his effort to fit the question to his answer. He then provided his prepared answer which was aimed at a specific targeted audience. In attempting to fit the questions to his answers, as Ritter and Henry note, Carter avoided answering over 40 percent of the questions asked him, though he clearly addressed his principal targeted audiences.

Thus, political debaters attain their goal of treating issues related to specifically targeted audiences first by utilizing the blocks of time over which they have complete control, their opening and closing addresses. Second, they often make the questions fit their answers by ignoring, twisting, or broadly interpreting questions in a manner which enables them to present an answer that strikes to the concerns of their targeted audiences.

The second issue-oriented goal of many candidates is to develop an overall theme. Two strategies have been frequently utilized to achieve this goal. First, candidates use their opening and closing remarks to express this theme and reaffirm it. Second, candidates consistently use their answers to each specific issue to reinforce this theme.

Dan Hahn has observed that, in 1992, Bush attempted to develop three issues in the initial debate. He sought to focus on Clinton as a tax-and-spend liberal, he sought to focus on Clinton as a man of questionable character who was unworthy of trust, and he sought to focus on his own experience and foreign policy success. Hence, Bush's message was not clearly focused around one central overarching theme. In contrast, both Clinton and Perot concentrated primarily on one theme which came across clearly. Clinton focused on the need for economic change, stressing that his proposals offered hope versus Bush's record of failure. Perot focused on his experience as a successful, can-do, no-nonsense businessman who would get this country moving, particularly economically, in contrast to conventional political backgrounds of his opponents who had contributed to many of our problems.

Similarly, in 1996, as Kendall and Ragsdale have illustrated, the Democratic candidates hewed closely to their overarching theme that they would balance the budget while protecting Medicare, Medicaid, education, and environment. This "mantra" became so common in the Clinton/Gore campaign that, as Ragsdale observed, it was referred to as "M2E2." During the debates it manifested itself in a variety of ways. As Kendall found, during the first debate, Clinton focused on the contrasting budget proposals of the candidates. On five occasions Clinton referred to Dole's proposal for a 15 percent across-the-board tax cut as a "tax scheme" in contrast to his own more limited and focused tax cuts which Clinton claimed would contribute to a balanced budget. Similarly, as Ragsdale has observed, Gore utilized this Democratic theme repeatedly, starting with his first two responses. In contrast, it was not until his fourth opportunity to speak that Kemp first mentioned his basic theme for the evening, that he and Dole wished to cut taxes across the board. Throughout the evening, Ragsdale suggests, Kemp was less focused than Gore, indeed even failing to mention his overall theme in his final statement.

Thus, the second issue-oriented goal of developing a broad, inclusive, overall theme with which most voters can identify is typically accomplished by national political debaters through the use of two strategies. First, they use their opening and closing remarks to present and reiterate their theme without interruptions or distractions from their opponents or the panel. Second, they consistently return to that theme with many of the specific answers they provide. Specific answers are used throughout the debate to constantly reinforce the overall theme presented in the opening speech.

The third issue-oriented goal of national political debaters is debating not to lose. The fear of failure which motivates this goal is a pervasive one among national political debaters. Consequently, the three strategies which are commonly used to avoid a fatal mistake are evident in virtually every national political debate.

The first strategy has already been examined. Debaters will ignore, twist, or broadly interpret questions to facilitate providing the answers they want to provide. This strategy, fitting the question to the answer, has already been discussed as a means of allowing candidates to address targeted audiences. In addition, it also serves to enable the candidate to fall back on frequently delivered past messages that have proven safe and uncontroversial. By fitting the dangerous question to the safe answer, the danger is removed and the candidate escapes the possibility of making a serious error.

The second strategy frequently used when debating not to lose is to avoid specifics. The candidate avoids indicting, or praising, any specific program or action, and rather speaks in generalities. Berquist characterized Jimmy Carter's overall strategy in 1976 as one of "issue avoidance," observing that Carter adhered to abstract statements of principles which generated little controversy. Carter's overall strategy in 1976 is a common one in the context of political debates, where candidates frequently avoid speaking in specifics which might offend some voters, and deliberately speak in generalities, which are unlikely to offend.

This tactic was particularly evident in the 1988 Bush-Dukakis debates, as Ryan elucidates throughout his study. Both men, for example, had difficulty in naming three weapons systems they would cut from the military budget. To do so would invite criticism and provoke controversy. No doubt the weapons systems so named would immediately be thoroughly investigated by both the press and their opponent. Perhaps those systems would be found to have value, and their elimination would be viewed as a grave mistake. But both men could safely indict our weapons procurement procedures. Both could also claim that they were well qualified to make the "tough choices" the next president would confront when the Pentagon budget came under review. Such indictments and claims were vague enough to be safe.

The final strategy widely utilized by candidates who are debating not to lose is to fall back on the stock responses they have utilized throughout the campaign. Because they have been used repeatedly in the past, such responses are safe. They involve no serious risk or gamble. It is impossible to calculate how often a response in a national political debate has been little more than a digest, often an exact repetition, of the candidate's stock response on an issue. The frequent press criticism of debates, that little new was offered by the candidates, attests to the widespread reliance candidates place on stock responses. Occasionally, as in 1988, when Dan Quayle repeated his comparison of himself to John Kennedy, or in 1992 when George Bush attacked Clinton's activities in Europe during the Vietnam era, stock issues and responses may backfire. The opponent may be ready for them, as was Bentsen for Quayle and Clinton for Bush. Or, they may not work as well with a national audience as they have worked in front of largely sympathetic partisan audiences in the primaries, at the convention, and elsewhere. Nevertheless, for the most part, candidates who are debating not to lose will rely heavily on the tried and true responses of the past. Rarely will they venture forth with new and novel ideas.

As these essays have illustrated, national political debates are high stakes games. Candidates and their staffs typically fear failure and a principal goal frequently becomes not to lose. This goal frequently prompts the use of three strategies. The first is to fit the question to the answer, enabling candidates to treat the topics they wish to treat, rather than those upon which they are questioned. The second is to avoid specifics. Inherent in responding to questions specifically is the possibility of making a mistake, of committing an error, which in the glare of a national political debate might result in losing. Finally, candidates rarely offer new ideas in national political debates. Rather, they repeat stock responses that have been frequently used on the campaign trail. When debating not to lose, such responses are particularly inviting.

Image-Oriented Strategies

As indicated earlier, typically national political debaters have one or more of four image-related goals. To attain the two positive goals: creating a positive image of themselves or positively modifying their existing image, or to attain the two negative goals: creating a negative image of their opponent or negatively modifying their opponent's existing image, candidates utilize a variety of strategies.

Many scholars and practitioners have commented upon image-oriented strategies.[20] The essays in this volume illustrate many of the more common image strategies. Positive image goals are commonly implemented by utilizing four strategies. Candidates seeking to create or enhance their own image in a positive fashion typically try to (1) present themselves as vigorous, active leaders, (2) foster identification of themselves with national aspirations, (3) foster identification of themselves with the dominant political party/philosophy, and (4) personify themselves as exemplifying a desirable characteristic.

First, most candidates seek to create an image of themselves as experienced, activist leaders who take charge of events, rather than as passive leaders who respond to events. In 1980, both

Carter and Reagan attempted to portray themselves as activist leaders. Carter constantly reminded the audience of his many actions as president, claiming that "I've made thousands of decisions.... We initiated.... We are now planning." Likewise, Reagan reminded the audience that he was an activist leader, claiming that "I have submitted.... I have opposed.... I stood. ... As Governor when I."

Similarly, in his opening statement during the first 1996 debate, Clinton portrayed himself as an activist, claiming of his administration, "We cut the deficit.... We cut taxes.... We passed family and medical leave.... We passed 100,000 new police.... We passed welfare reform." Not only did Clinton point to his first-term activities, but as he cited each of these accomplishments he commented on how he would continue acting in his second term. "Now let's pass the tax cuts.... Now let's expand it.... Now let's keep going by.... Now let's move a million people.... Most important.... Let's make education." Clearly Clinton portrayed himself as an activist president during his first term who would continue to be an activist in his second term.

Often, as with the cases of Kennedy in 1960, Reagan in 1980, Bush and Ferraro in 1984, and Quayle in 1988, the efforts of the candidates to project their leadership qualities may well be the most important aspect of the debate. Kennedy and Reagan had great success in this regard in 1960 and 1980, making themselves dramatically more acceptable to the public as potential presidents. As all of the studies of vice presidential debates have noted, an important consideration of virtually all of the vice presidential debaters was to portray themselves as strong leaders, able to assume the mantle of the presidency if that occasion arose.

Vice presidential candidate Dan Quayle had difficulty in projecting leadership both in 1988 and again in 1992. In 1988, as Decker has observed, Quayle's delivery was marked by repeated hesitancies which did much to deny his claims to be a decisive leader. Moreover, his repeated inabilities to indicate how he would first respond if he had to assume the presidency also worked to undermine claims that he was prepared to lead. In 1992, he handled the question about his qualifications to be President much better than he had responded to the analogous question in 1988. However, as Devlin's study illustrates, Quayle's often disjointed interruptions, his less-dignified gesturing, his sometimes ill-timed smiles, and his sometimes shrill delivery all undermined his attempts to project his leadership ability.

A second strategy candidates commonly use to create a positive image is to identify themselves with the principal aspirations of their audience. As Ritter and Henry have illustrated, Reagan was exceptionally effective at this in 1980, particularly in his closing remarks when he presented himself as the candidate who could best improve the nation's economy. During his closing remarks in the second 1984 debate, with an economy much improved over that of 1980 (or at least not as vulnerable to attack, since he had been the major player in shaping economic policy for the preceding four years), Reagan chose to identify with our national aspirations to maintain peace and the natural environment. Clinton was also highly effective in his 1996 attempt to identify himself with the national aspirations for an improved educational system that would provide a bright future for our children.

A third strategy candidates commonly use to create a positive image is to identify themselves with a party or philosophy. Because nationally, until recently, the Democratic Party has been larger than the Republican Party, Democratic candidates have consistently attempted to identify themselves with their party. In 1960, Kennedy went out of his way, as Windt illustrates, to mention the major constituent groups of the party in his opening remarks. Throughout the debates he repeatedly identified himself as the heir to the Democratic Party tradition.

Clearly this strategy was not available to Republican candidates. As Windt notes, in 1960 Richard Nixon actively avoided identifying himself with the Republican Party. However, by 1980 Ronald Reagan had co-opted the Democratic strategy of identifying with the party by instead identifying with philosophy. Reagan identified himself with the majority conservative philosophy that encompassed Republicans and disaffected Democrats. In 1988, George Bush similarly identified himself with the majority conservative philosophy. He did so again in 1992, though perhaps with lesser effect, since Clinton was not as clearly liberal as Dukakis had been.

By 1996, with the Republicans triumphant in the 1994 congressional elections, Senator Dole used the opening statement of the first debate to twice remind Republicans that he was the nominee of their party, though unlike many of his Republican predecessors, he did not comment on the conservative philosophy widely credited with the party's success. Thus, whether it be identification with party or philosophy, often national political debaters will attempt to shape their image through identification.

Finally, debaters will attempt to positively influence their images by suggesting that they personify characteristics or roles that the public seeks in the president. As Berquist notes, Jimmy Carter built his entire 1976 campaign around personifying honesty, trustworthiness, and managerial competency. As the essays in this volume indicate, in 1996, both Clinton and Gore stressed their managerial competency. Ragsdale observes, for example, that both Kemp and Gore attempted to convey their leadership abilities through the use of action-oriented language, though he finds that Gore was the more successful.

The principal negative image strategy is to attack the opponent, attempting to tarnish his/her image. Typically, the attacks focus around the same strategies as the positive image-building strategies. John Kennedy attacked the leadership of the Eisenhower-Nixon administration, claiming that America could accomplish more. Jimmy Carter attacked the leadership of the Nixon-Ford administration, claiming that America deserved more ethical leadership. Ronald Reagan attacked the Carter administration's ability to lead us out of our economic difficulties and to lead the free world.

John Kennedy and virtually every national Democratic candidate since have sought to identify their opponent as a Republican, presumably a candidate from the party of wealth, who consequently could have no sympathy for the middle and lower classes. In 1996, the Democrats argued for a "focused" tax cut, focused upon the lower and middle classes, as opposed to Dole's 15 percent across-the-board tax cuts and the Dole/Kemp calls for capital gains tax relief, both of which would benefit the wealthy as well as the middle and perhaps lower class.

By 1976, Robert Dole was indicting Walter Mondale as the "most liberal member of the United States Senate," attacking philosophy rather than party. Ronald Reagan and George Bush continued this Republican assault on their respective opponents, seeking to identify them not as Democrats but as liberals. As Kendall and Ragsdale illustrate, Kemp attempted to pursue this attack more vigorously than Dole, while both Clinton and Gore spoke primarily to their pragmatic accomplishments, rather than underlying philosophical beliefs. Hence, negative attempts to tarnish an opponent's image reflect the same basic strategies as positive attempts to build one's own image. But rather than focus constructively on oneself, negative strategies consist primarily of attacking the leadership style, identification, and personification, of one's opponent.

Post-Debate Strategies

National political debaters seemed to have learned much from the second 1976 debate, best remembered because President Ford seemed to be unaware of the Soviet domination of Eastern Europe. Importantly, as Berquist points out, Ford was not perceived to have erred when he first made that remark. It was not until the next day, by which time the media had focused on this remark, that the public began to perceive it as a serious mistake. Consequently, today post-debate strategy focuses on providing a massive and well-coordinated surrogate effort. Prominent spokespersons for the candidate are made readily accessible to the media. Not only do they suggest that their candidate won, but often they have been alerted in advance to stress key themes in their analyses. Research suggests that audience members often do not make their judgment on the outcome of the debate until they have talked with others and observed media reaction.[21] It is during this crucial period of time, shortly after the debate and through the next few news cycles, that the campaign attempts to affect audience perceptions.

As Kendall illustrates, in 1996 the media provided viewers

with the remarks of a variety of figures in their post-debate shows. Significantly, though the vice presidential candidates were utilized on these shows, as Kendall illustrates, the networks tended to rely primarily on their own reporters and print journalists. In 1996 the networks largely ignored partisan surrogates in their post-debate shows.

DEBATE EFFECTS

Perhaps no other aspect of political debating has been subjected to as much study as the effects of political debates. As each of these studies has indicated, after each debate, public opinion polls attempt to measure the impact of the debate on voter attitudes. Columnists and political commentators utilize polls and anecdotal evidence to speculate about the consequences of the debate. And, of course, scholars from a variety of disciplines including political science, journalism, and communication utilize a wide variety of methodologies to examine the effects of political debates. That material is widely available and it would serve little point to thoroughly review it here.[22] Suffice it to say that the Kendall and Ragsdale studies of the 1996 debates confirm the findings of prior studies that the principal effect of political debates is to reinforce, rather than shift, voter attitudes. Debates do shift some voters. In some campaigns, most notably those of 1960 and 1980, the debates may have altered the votes of significant numbers of voters. Nevertheless, the principal effect of debates upon voting behavior seems to be to reinforce the existing attitudes of voters.

However, it should be remembered that debates do have a variety of effects in addition to simply helping voters make up their minds. National political debates help to educate our citizens. National political debates help to reinforce our open democratic heritage. National political debates help to socialize our young people. National political debates help to legitimize the transference of power from one administration to another. All of these positive effects that national political debates have on our society clearly justify the continuation of some form of national political debates.[23]

FUTURE OF POLITICAL DEBATES

Critics have often questioned either the format of a particular debate or the questions asked by the journalists. A variety of formats have been used in national political debates. A variety of means have been used in selecting the panelists.[24] Most criticism of debate formats claims that they impede the public's learning. Most criticism of the journalists' questions suggests that they too impede the public's learning, by virtue of their focus on trite or inappropriate issues.

While such criticism has merit, it frequently seems to be offered without consideration of the rhetorical situation that governs political debates. From the standpoint of the participants, the motivating exigence is not the desire to educate the public. It is the desire to win the election. From the standpoint of the panel journalists, the motivating exigence is not the desire to educate the public. It is the desire to create a newsworthy event. Hence, none of the participants in national political debates is highly motivated to provide an educational experience for the viewer.

Given that the basic motivation of each candidate is incompatible with the basic motivation of the opponent, and given that debating not to lose, a major strategy of most national political debaters, is clearly incompatible with the desires of the panelists, it should certainly not surprise us that decisions about formats and panels, as well as a variety of other factors, are made through negotiation.

Recent debates have been sponsored by the non-partisan Commission on Presidential Debates, which was established in 1987 specifically to sponsor presidential debates, in recognition of the educational value they offer.[25] However, as 1996 well illustrated, though the Commission may well represent the public's interests, the strongest hands at the bargaining table are held by the candidates. Without their participation there is no debate. In recent years, as we have seen, public pressure for debate has largely eliminated the once viable option that national candidates had of refusing to seriously consider debating. To this extent the hand of the public, as represented through the Commission, has been strengthened. However, the details of format and panel selection, as well as a host of other variables, such as the number and length of the debates, the topics to be covered, and the presence and role of a live audience, are all subject to negotiation. Consequently, we must expect that at least for the foreseeable future, decisions made on subjects such as these will be compromise decisions.

Compromise decisions are not necessarily bad. Few would argue that the public has been ill-served by national political debates. Democracies are nothing if they are not compromise. Indeed, the virtue of democracy is that each voice counts. When voices offset one another with opposing attitudes and interests, negotiation and compromise ensues. The results typically do not satisfy everyone perfectly. Rather they reflect the constraints of the situation, typically enabling all participants to derive at least some benefit. To the extent that political debates are a uniquely Democratic experience, why should we expect them to differ?

NOTES

1. Robert V. Friedenberg, ed., *Rhetorical Studies of National Political Debates: 1960–1992* (Westport, Conn.: Praeger, 1994).

2. This and all subsequent references to characteristics of the 1960 presidential debates are drawn from Theodore Windt, "The 1960 Kennedy-Nixon Presidential Debates," in *Rhetorical Studies of National Political Debates: 1960–1992*, ed. Robert V. Friedenberg (Westport, Conn.: Praeger, 1994), pp. 1–28.

3. This and all subsequent references to characteristics of the 1976 presidential debates are drawn from Goodwin Berquist, "The 1976 Carter-Ford Presidential Debates," in *Rhetorical Studies of National Political Debates: 1960–1992*, ed. Robert V. Friedenberg (Westport, Conn.: Praeger, 1994), pp. 29–44.

4. This and all subsequent references to characteristics of the 1980 presidential debates are drawn from Kurt Ritter and David Henry, "The 1980 Reagan-Carter Presidential Debate," in *Rhetorical Studies of National Political Debates: 1960–1992*, ed. Robert V. Friedenberg (Westport, Conn.: Praeger, 1994), pp. 69–95.

5. This and all subsequent references to characteristics of the 1976 vice presidential debates are drawn from Kevin Sauter, "The 1976 Mondale-Dole Vice Presidential Debate," in *Rhetorical Studies of National Political Debates: 1960–1992*, ed. Robert V. Friedenberg (Westport, Conn.: Praeger, 1994), pp. 45–68.

6. This and all subsequent references to characteristics of the 1984 presidential debates are drawn from Craig Allen Smith and Kathy B. Smith, "The 1984 Reagan-Mondale Presidential Debates," in *Rhetorical Studies of National Political Debates: 1960–1992*, ed. Robert V. Friedenberg (Westport, Conn.: Praeger, 1994), pp. 95–120.

7. Donald Morrison, ed., *The Winning of the White House: 1988* (New York: Time Books, 1988), p. 258.

8. Myles Martel, *Political Campaign Debates: Images Strategies and Tactics* (New York: Longman and Company, 1983), p. 58.

9. This and all subsequent references to characteristics of the 1988 presidential debates are drawn from Halford Ryan, "The 1988 Bush-Dukakis Presidential Debates," in *Rhetorical Studies of National Political Debates: 1960–1992*, ed. Robert V. Friedenberg (Westport, Conn.: Praeger, 1994), pp. 145–166.

10. This and all subsequent references to characteristics of the 1992 presidential debates are drawn from Dan F. Hahn, "The 1992 Clinton-Bush-Perot Presidential Debates," in *Rhetorical Studies of National Political Debates: 1960–1992*, ed. Robert V. Friedenberg (Westport, Conn.: Praeger, 1994), pp. 187–210.

This and all subsequent references to characteristics of the 1992 vice presidential debates are drawn from L. Patrick Devlin, "The 1992 Gore-Quayle-Stockdale Vice Presidential Debates," in *Rhetorical Studies of National Political Debates: 1960–1992*, ed. Robert V. Friedenberg (Westport, Conn.: Praeger, 1994), pp. 211–234.

11. See the studies of the vice presidential debates in Friedenberg, *Rhetorical Studies of National Political Debates: 1960–1992*.

12. This and all subsequent references to characteristics of the 1984 vice presidential debate are drawn from Judith Trent, "The 1984 Bush-Ferraro Vice Presidential Debate," in *Rhetorical Studies of National Political Debates: 1960–1992*, ed. Robert V. Friedenberg (Westport, Conn.: Praeger, 1994), pp. 121–144.

13. This and all subsequent references to characteristics of the 1988 vice presidential debate are drawn from Warren Decker, "The 1988 Quayle-Bentsen Vice Presidential Debate," in *Rhetorical Studies of National Political Debates: 1960–1992*, ed. Robert V. Friedenberg (Westport, Conn.: Praeger, 1994), pp. 167–186.

14. Robert O. Weiss, "The Presidential Debates in Their Political Context: The Issue-Image Interface in the 1980 Campaign," *Speaker and Gavel* 18 (Winter 1981): 22.

15. Myles Martel, *Political Campaign Debates*, p. 78.

16. See Martel, *Political Campaign Debates*, pp. 78–83 for an exceptionally informed description of Reagan's preparation in this regard.

17. See Goodwin F. Berquist and James L. Golden, "Media Rhetoric, Criticism, and the Public Perception of the 1980 Presidential Debates," *Quarterly Journal of Speech* 67 (May 1981): 125–137 for an insightful analysis of the dynamics between the candidates, their staffs, and the media, that helps to create public expectations.

18. Kennedy intimates such as his brother Robert and longtime aid Kenneth O'Donnell felt that the 1960 debates were, in many respects, a "rerun" of Kennedy's 1952 debate with Lodge. See Kenneth P. O'Donnell and David F. Powers, *Johnny, We Hardly Knew Ye* (New York: Pocket Books, 1973), pp. 103–104, 243–244. Inexplicably, I am aware of no evidence that Lodge forewarned Nixon about Kennedy's debating skills.

19. Virtually all of the references which were more salient to men involved the economy. Those that were more salient to women included four references to health care issues, four references to education, and three to families and child rearing.

20. Two of the better such discussions are those of Dan Nimmo, *Popular Images of Politics* (Englewood Cliffs, N.J.: Prentice-Hall, 1974), pp. 102–104; and Martel, *Political Campaign Debates*, pp. 62–75.

21. Frederick T. Steeper, "Public Response to Gerald Ford's Statements on Eastern Europe in the Second Debate," in *The Presidential Debates: Media, Electoral, and Policy Perspectives*, ed. George F. Bishop, Robert G. Meadow, and Marilyn Jackson-Beeck (New York: Praeger, 1978), p. 101; Roger Desmond and Thomas Donohue, "The Role of the 1976 Televised Presidential Debates in the Political Socialization of Adolescents," *Communication Quarterly* 29 (Summer 1981): 306–308; and George A. Barnett, "A Multidimensional Analysis of the 1976 Presidential Campaign," *Communication Quarterly* 29 (Summer 1981): 156–165.

22. Many of the books and articles cited in the individual chapter bibliographies in *Rhetorical Studies of National Political Debates: 1960–1992*, ed. Robert V. Friedenberg, discuss the effects of a specific debate. For overviews of the effects of political debating, see Judith S. Trent and Robert V. Friedenberg, *Political Campaign Communication: Principles and Practices*, 3rd ed. (Westport, Conn.: Praeger, 1995), pp. 228–236; and Sidney Kraus, *Televised Presidential Debates and Public Policy* (Hillsdale, N.J.: Lawrence Erlbaum Associates, 1988), pp. 103–134.

23. This is not to suggest that the flaws currently associated with national political debate cannot be corrected. For cogent suggestions about improving future debates, see Kathleen Hall Jamieson and David S. Birdsell, *Presidential Debates: The Challenge of Creating An Informed Electorate* (New York: Oxford University Press, 1988), pp. 194–221. Also see Kraus, *Televised Presidential Debates and Public Policy*, pp. 135–160.

24. See Martel, *Political Campaign Debates*, pp. 126–132, for a discussion of the selection process and the role of panelists in political debates. Additionally, see pp. 116–150 of Martel for an exceedingly thorough discussion of debate formats. Kraus also presents highly informed discussions of debate formats, as well as the selection and role of panelists. See Kraus, *Televised Presidential Debates and Public Policy*, pp. 29–72, and 135–160.

25. Commission on Presidential Debates, "A Viewer's Guide to Political Debates" (Washington D.C.: Commission on Presidential Debates, 1992), p. 4.

Select Bibliography on Political Campaign Debating

At the conclusion of Chapters 1 and 2 of this volume the reader can find a select annotated bibliography that focuses on the specific debate examined in that chapter. Additionally, the chapter bibliographies provide the reader with sources for debate transcripts and audio/video recordings. Thus, this bibliography excludes all works that focus exclusively or heavily on either the presidential or vice presidential debates of 1996. Rather, it presents works which treat the genre of political debating, particularly at the presidential level.

BOOKS

Benoit, William L., and William T. Wells. *Candidates in Conflict: Persuasive Attack and Defense in the 1992 Presidential Debates.* Tuscaloosa: University of Alabama Press, 1996. This book is an outgrowth of the first author's studies of the strategies of persuasive attack and persuasive defense. The authors offer a new perspective for examining debates by focusing on strategies designed to damage an image, and those designed to repair an image. They examine the 1992 presidential debates from this perspective.

Commission on Presidential Debates. "Review of 1992 Presidential Debates." Washington D.C.: Freedom Forum, 1993. Six months after the 1992 debates, many of the participants, including the moderators and campaign debate coordinators for each of the candidates, participated in a day-long debriefing which treated such topics as how the moderators handled themselves, the debate negotiations between the Commission and the respective campaigns, viewer reaction to the debates, and a host of other topics. This is the transcript of those meetings.

Friedenberg, Robert V., ed. *Rhetorical Studies of National Political Debates: 1960–1992.* New York: Praeger, 1994. Chapter-length studies treat each of the presidential and vice presidential debates held between 1960 and 1992 in the companion volume to this work. Each chapter examines such topics as candidate motivation to debate, the goals, rhetorical strategies, and effects of the debates. The concluding chapter focuses on patterns and trends in national political debating.

Hellweg, Susan A., Michael Pfau, and Steven R. Brydon. *Televised Presidential Debates: Advocacy in Contemporary America.* New York: Praeger, 1992. After an opening chapter detailing the history of television involvement in debates, the authors focus on the formats of debates and the interaction between the visual and vocal dimensions of debates.

Jamieson, Kathleen Hall, and David S. Birdsell. *Presidential Debates: The Challenge of Creating An Informed Electorate.* New York: Oxford University Press, 1988. The first three chapters constitute the best short history of American political debating prior to the broadcast age. The remainder of this excellent study focuses on the impact of broadcasting on political debates, the problems broadcasting has created, and suggestions for future political debates.

Kraus, Sidney. *Televised Presidential Debates and Public Policy.* Hillsdale, N.J.: Lawrence Erlbaum Associates, 1988. An excellent study which treats such topics as the role of television in presidential elections, formats for televised debates, media coverage of debates, and the impact of televised debates. Concludes with a discussion of policy options for future presidential debates.

Martel, Myles. *Political Campaign Debates: Images, Strategies, and Tactics.* New York: Longman, 1983. Still among the best examinations of political debate strategies available. Martel's study is based heavily on his own experiences as a political debate coach to a variety of candidates, and his interviews with over one hundred candidates, advisors, network officials, journalists, and others.

Swerdlow, Joel L., ed. *Presidential Debates: 1988 and Beyond.* Washington, D.C.: Congressional Quarterly Press, 1988. The editor's history of political debates as well as survey and other data on political debates dating back to 1948 makes this a valuable reference work for those interested in political debates. Sponsored by the League of Women Voters, this volume also features a selection of six essays treating the sponsorship of political debates.

ARTICLES/CHAPTERS

Drucker, Susan J., and Janice Platt Hunold. "The Debating Game." *Critical Studies in Mass Communication* 4 (1987): 202–207. A disturbing and thought-provoking critique which argues that in substance, style, and audience perception, political debates are already highly analogous to television game shows and likely to move even more toward entertaining television rather than bona fide news events.

Faucheux, Ron. "Debate Watcher's Guide." *Campaigns and Elections* (October/November 1996): 28–32. This article provides the reader with one former consultant's basis for evaluating political debates. Faucheux is editor of *Campaigns and Elections* and his "Scorecard," included in this article, involves evaluating the strategic adaptations of the debaters to the debate situation, as well as a host of delivery-related criteria.

Friedenberg, Robert V. "The 1992 Presidential Debates." In *The 1992 Presidential Campaign: A Communication Perspective*, ed. Robert Denton. Westpost, Conn.: Praeger, 1994, pp. 89–110. This study examines all three of the 1992 presidential debates utilizing seven criteria the author has found to be characteristic of successful political debaters. It also treats the decision to debate and offers observations on the varying formats used in the 1992 debates.

Friedenberg, Robert V. " 'We Are Present Here Today for the Purpose of Having a Joint Discussion': The Conditions Requisite for Political Debates." *Journal of the American Forensics Association* 16 (1979): 1–9. Claims that candidates agree to debate out of self-interest and posits six conditions necessary for candidates to agree to debate.

Friedenberg, Robert V. " 'Selfish Interests' or the Prerequisites for Political Debate: An Analysis of the 1980 Presidential Debate and Its Implications for Future Campaigns," *Journal of the American Forensics Association* 18 (1981): 91–98. Extends the author's prior examination of candidate motivation to debate and suggests that the institutionalization of presidential debates is at hand.

Lang, Gladys Engel. "Still Seeking Answers." *Critical Studies in Mass*

Communication 4 (1987): 211–213. Finds that in addition to their potential effect on voting decisions, political debates may have positive effects on the conduct of political campaigns, the ease presidents have in governing, and the public image of politics. Lang also notes that debates may foster citizens to behave as spectators of, rather than participants in, political events.

Meadow, Robert G. "A Speech By Any Other Name." *Critical Studies in Mass Communication* 4 (1987): pp. 207–210. Argues that debates do not contribute to the election dialogue and claims that the pressure for political debates comes from the very group which benefits from debates, journalists.

Morello, John T. "The 'Look' and Language of Clash: Visual Structuring of Argument in the 1988 Bush-Dukakis Debates." *The Southern Communication Journal* 57 (1992): 205–218. Through use of the 1988 debate as a case study, this work illustrates the importance of the visual shoots used during televised debates, arguing that they clearly transmute the process of argument in a debate.

Murphy, John M. "Presidential Debates and Campaign Rhetoric: Text Within Context." *The Southern Communication Journal* 57 (1992): 219–228. A well-written study that argues that political debates must be viewed in the context of the entire campaign to be fully understood. Uses the 1968 California primary debate between Robert Kennedy and Eugene McCarthy as a case study.

Owen, Diana. "The Debate Challenge." In *Presidential Campaign Discourse*, ed. Kathleen Kendall. Albany: State University of New York Press, 1995, pp. 135–156. Owen perceives presidential debates to be media events. Consequently, she focuses heavily on media treatment of debate negotiation, the media strategies candidates use in preparing for the debates, and post-debate media strategies, as well as the debates themselves.

Ritter, Kurt, and Susan A. Hellweg. "Televised Presidential Primary Debates: A New National Forum for Political Debating." *Journal of the American Forensic Association* 23 (1986): 1–14. An insightful examination of the history and growth in importance of televised presidential primary debates from 1956 to 1984.

Trent, Judith S., and Robert V. Friedenberg. "Debates in Political Campaigns." Chapter 8 of *Political Campaign Communication: Principles and Practices*, 3rd ed. Westport, Conn.: Praeger, 1995, pp. 209–243. An overview of the history, strategies, and effects of political debates.

Vancil, David L., and Sue D. Pendell. "Winning Presidential Debates: An Analysis of Criteria Influencing Audience Response." *The*

Western Journal of Speech Communication 48 (Winter 1984): 62–74. The authors argue that at least six criteria exist which audiences use to determine who won a presidential debate. This is an excellent short analysis of the complexity involved in determining political debate winners.

DEBATE TRANSCRIPTS AND VIDEOTAPES

Each of the individual chapter bibliographies includes sources for the transcripts of the 1996 debates. The best depositories for videotapes of national political debates are the Vanderbilt Television News Archive, Vanderbuilt University Library, Vanderbilt University, Nashville, Tennessee, 37240; and the C-Span Archives affiliated with Purdue University which can be contacted at 22 N. Second Street, P.O. Box 620, Lafayette, IN 47902, or (800) 277–2698.

Index

About the Contributors

ROBERT V. FRIEDENBERG (Ph.D. Temple University) is Professor of Communication at Miami (Ohio) University. He is editor of *Rhetorical Studies of National Political Debates: 1960–1992* (Praeger, 1994) and co-author, with Judith S. Trent, of *Political Campaign Communication: Principles and Practices* (Praeger, 1995). He has also authored *Theodore Roosevelt and the Rhetoric of Militant Decency* (Greenwood, 1990) and *Hear O' Israel: The History of American Jewish Preaching 1654–1970* (1989). He is currently working on a book which will examine communication consultants in political campaigns.

KATHLEEN E. KENDALL is Associate Professor of Communication, University at Albany, State University of New York. She has published *Presidential Campaign Discourse: Strategic Communication Problems* (1995) and articles in journals such as *American Behavioral Scientist, Communication Quarterly,* and *Presidential Studies Quarterly.* Her research interests focus on political campaign communication, particularly the interaction of the candidates and the media, and the study of presidential primaries.

She regularly assists the Albany area media with their political coverage.

GAUT RAGSDALE is Associate Professor of Communication at Northern Kentucky University where he teaches political communication, persuasion, and organizational communication. His research interests include political communication and corporate advocacy. He is a certified parliamentarian and serves as parliamentarian to several national organizations, including the National Education Association.